MW00903197

# THROUGH SOUL'S EYES

## REINVENTING A LIFE OF JOY AND PROMISE

JANE A. SIMINGTON, PH.D

YWCA
Woman of
Distinction

Global TV
Woman of
Vision

# OTHER WORKS BY
# JANE A. SIMINGTON, PH.D

*Books*

*Journey to the Sacred: Mending a Fractured Soul*
*Setting the Captive Free*
*Viaje Hacia Lo Sagrado*

*Booklet*

*Responding Soul to Soul: During Times of Spiritual Uprooting*

*DVDs*

*Listening to Soul Pain*
*Healing Soul Pain*

*CDs*

*Journey to Healing; Connecting with Healing Light*
*Cloaked in Joy: Your Guide to Release Hurt and Claim Joy*
*Shielded With Light: A Guide for Cleansing and Sealing Your Aura*
*Releasing Ties That Bind: Your Guide for Cutting Energy Cords*
    *and Attachments*
*Reintegrating Parts of the Self*
*Retrieving Lost Soul Parts.*

# FOREWORD

I vividly recall the first words I ever said to Dr. Jane Simington. "I would speak to you about my soul," I said this, with utter clarity and conviction. And yet, I did not know her at all; we had not conversed, and I had not heard her speak in the workshop in which we were fellow participants. She and I had been asked to sit together in silence for 10 minutes and then tell the other what we would like to talk about. At the time, I didn't understand where my words came from, but now I recognize that it was my soul's longing that inspired my words. It was as though my soul knew that knowing Jane would change my life's path and that this connection would further my life's purpose. That moment of clarity was an awakening for me, a continuation and expansion of my ongoing sacred journey of discovery.

I was compelled to again connect with Jane after the workshop concluded—compelled with an intensity I had never before experienced. I explained to her on the telephone that I needed to know her, but that I didn't know why. It was then that she told me that she worked in the fields of grief support and trauma recovery and that much of her work was with the First Nation's people of Canada. To satisfy my need for connection with her, I agreed that it was important, for me, to attend her Trauma Recovery Certification training program.

Prior to the training I delved into Jane's book, *Journey to the Sacred: Mending the Fractured Soul*. This book, as the title suggests, is about Jane's journey into despair after the tragic death of her son and her subsequent search for ways to heal her broken spirit. Her story touched me deeply, at many levels. I knew that she was a pioneer of sorts—she dared to speak the truth about pain and speak the truth about the miserable failure of our society to meet someone at the place of their pain. As I read, I underlined and hi-lighted much of the book, often peppering the air with exclamations of "Yes!"

I learned from Jane's teachings that when human beings experience trauma, a profound spiritual disconnection occurs. We lose parts of our soul, and along with those parts we lose, amongst other things, the capacity to trust, the ability to feel safe, and the sense that we can believe in ourselves and others. We disconnect from our Divine Source. When weighted down with trauma and grief, we live in fear, unable to claim our voices, unable to heal our pain.

From Jane I learned about the physiology of trauma and how our healing must happen primarily in our right brain, where we can access and process our traumatic experiences. I learned of the great importance of the lessons from the ancient ones; the value of sacred ceremony and ritual, our primal connection to the elements, the healing powers of the drum, song and dance, guided imagery and journey work, movement, journaling, and sharing. I began to grasp the necessity of moving to a new paradigm if we are to work successfully with trauma and grief. This new paradigm provides the gift of the sure knowledge that if we are to heal trauma, we must not only speak of spiritual connection; we must also create the opportunity for spiritual connection for those who live with trauma and grief. It is this gift of spiritual connection that I have witnessed over and over again as Jane shares her teachings and her experience.

I have been privileged to work with Jane as she facilitates the healing work of both trauma recovery and grief support. This training enables individuals to work with others who seek healing. She is passionate about sharing her knowledge, her wisdom, her experience, and her many gifts so that others might be free from the bondage created by unhealed trauma and grief. She provides a holistic approach to healing and welcomes each person's wholeness and magnificence. Jane is utterly fearless as she holds her truth out for anyone who might like to try it on for size. But never will she ask you to accept her truth as your own; rather, she will encourage you to enter into your own experience, knowing that it is only from within your own experience that you will find what is true for you.

It is with great courage and great calm that Jane is able to hold another's deepest pain. She provides safety and compassion, creating the opportunity for each individual to find their own path to healing. I have learned from her what it means to be filled with gratitude for the help and guidance we can each receive from the spirit world.

In this beautifully written book, Jane shares her wisdom and her experience, and she asks that we carefully consider the absolute and urgent need for each one of us to seek healing and wholeness, not only for ourselves, but for our loved ones and for our Earth. She provides us with many thought-provoking insights and encourages us to ponder them. She offers us a feast of activities, exercises, guided imageries, and art experiences that enhance the wondrous journey to connection and wholeness. I invite you to honour yourself as you set aside precious time and sacred space to travel the path from captivity to freedom.

*Gail Barrett, MA, RCC*

# TABLE OF CONTENTS

# INTRODUCTION

We have entered a new age, an age in which old ways of being and doing no longer serve. This new age has ushered in a higher level of energy, an energy that resonates deep within our being—reawakening us to our true essence—our spiritual essence. *Through Soul's Eyes* challenges you to question the status quo of your life and life circumstances, and invites you to examine your reality as viewed through your soul's eyes. In doing so, you expand your consciousness and therefore your abilities to see and function beyond the physical boundaries. This level of being supports powerful and positive change in numerous aspects of your life and your relationships—both personal and professional relationships.

The higher frequency energies now penetrating our world allows for healing and transformation at a rate and to a depth that was not possible a decade past. *Through Soul's Eyes* is a trusted resource in your search for ways to release all emotional and soul pain, from whatever the causes, and to know the freedom of living a life that is peace-filled and successful.

In each chapter of *Through Soul's Eyes* I clearly outline the techniques I have developed and used to heal and transform my own life after trauma and the lives of thousands of others from many cultures and from various parts of the world. I provide easy to follow directions for using each of the methods and include activities for you to complete and then reflect upon. I show you how to cross over the physical threshold and enter the level of your own soul, there to heal spiritual disconnection and welcome spiritual transformation. I provide the key to unlock and positively alter any difficult and even damaging messages stored in your brain, thus giving you the tools to heal your body, mind, emotions and soul and I share with you numerous stories of how these methods have helped to transform thousands of lives.

Are you searching for ways to change and transform—how to live the life you have always knew you were meant to live, to live a meaningful, abundant and purposeful life, one filled with joy and promise? If that is true, than *Through Soul's Eyes* is your guide.

I am honored to be of assistance as you journey toward inner freedom!

*Dr. Jane A. Simington, PhD.*

# CHAPTER 1

# EXPERIENCING PARALLEL REALITIES

*Everything in this world has a hidden meaning.*
*Men, animals, trees, stars, they are all hieroglyphics.*

Nikos Kazantzakis, *Zorba the Greek*

It was five in the morning when the news came. It was the only time the telephone had rung during my entire sojourn, and its sudden interruption of the stillness jarred me to full consciousness. Feeling an intense need for the soothing that only the ocean's waves can provide I quickly dressed and left my rented Balinese quarters. Intuition directed that I walk east—the direction of new beginnings.

My instinctive response to the difficult news was to send healing energy to my mother, hoping it would aid in curing her cancerous tumor. Yet even before I could fully formulate the intention, my attention was drawn to the magnificence unfolding before me. Mesmerized, I gazed as a large white bird elegantly lifted from the ocean's surface, to be followed by another of its kind. In a splendorous display of graceful ease the pair ascended upward and eastward, until they were gently immersed in the golden radiance of the morning sunrise.

Stillness followed and, in its glow, awareness. A sacred union was unfolding before me. I knew at a deep level, yet without a cognitive doubt that I was being privileged to witness circumstances as viewed from another level of reality. The powerful symbolism revealed in those extraordinary moments imprinted upon my soul a knowing that my father had come to accompany my mother and guide her journey homeward.

In most ancient societies, people studied the natural world to understand the supernatural. This knowledge, and the resulting beliefs, lingers within many cultures. One common belief is that spiritual guides use animals or animal imagery to communicate with humans. Birds are considered messengers from the spirit world. Through personal experiences, as well as through the observations of the spiritual growth of others, I came to recognize that, as we awaken to the spiritual aspects of ourselves, we automatically reawaken to the powerful spiritual messages being offered to us in the many forms that nature takes. We begin to recognize that colors and numbers are significant, and we come to know that nothing happens to us in this reality that does not have a mirrored reflection in and of the spiritual world.

As I gazed in awe, respect, and admiration at the magnificence being revealed, I recognized that I was given a powerful teaching. How could I witness such majesty, such splendor, feeling the joy of my parent's union, yet still desire to keep my mother in this dimension?

In that instance I knew my wish to send healing energies had little to do with my mother's best interest; rather, it was entirely about meeting my needs—my needs as a child, longing not to be orphaned. This acknowledgement shifted my intention. My prayer was no longer one of pleading for her life but was, instead, one of petition for her safe and easy passage to the other side. In that moment I chose not to hold my mother in captivity. I chose instead to free her of any bonds that might be between us, any bonds that would tie her to me and thus hold her in this reality. Mustering courage, I whispered, "With great love and gratitude for all you have given, for all you have taught, I now, in this moment, set you free. I wish you great joy as you advance on the next phase of your soul's journey."

The lesson was complete. The birds vanished. This sacred experience, like so many others, lasted but a moment, yet the effects continue to impact my soul to this day.

For a long time now I have been alert to the numerous and varied experiences that shaped my personal and professional life. I am aware of the powerful lessons I have had, and continue to have, that teach and reinforce my knowing: that we live and work and play in parallel universes, that during our Earth walk we have one foot in this reality and one in another dimension. I am also aware that in previous times I would not have noticed the splendorous birds that morning, or if I had noticed them, I would certainly not have acknowledged them as messengers from the spirit world.

I have, in recent times, also done considerable reflection on the reasons for my intense drive to acquire knowledge and gain skills in fields that appear to be (at least at first glance) unrelated. Yet my persistent spirit urges me forward. I continue to have a constant need to remind myself that I must walk in trust, because I believe that each of my experiences is necessary for the manifestation of some grander purpose. Although it is usually only in retrospect that I am able to identify the relationship between an adventure and the lessons it teaches me, at this point in my life I acknowledge that each discovery is somehow necessary for the next phase of my journey. I initially became profoundly aware of this when I began doing therapeutic work. Shortly after stepping fully into this aspect of practice, I recognized how frequently the person who had just left my office had taught me exactly what I needed to know and understand so that I might be of real assistance to the person who next sat beside me. The more that I was able to acknowledge, with gratitude, the teachings from the spiritual world, the more the guidance increased. It became awe inspiring to recognize that I was not alone—to know that I was being offered help to ensure a more positive, soulful outcome for the person who was seeking assistance for healing.

As I began to write this book, I knew which concepts and ideas I wanted to convey, yet because of my varied life experiences, I pondered the fit. What was the common thread? What was the theme? How, as a storyteller, could I convey in written form the images, the truths that surface from my own soulful experiences and the soulful experiences of those I walk beside?

I learned to rely on the powers of meditation and stillness to provide answers. Over the past decades I have walked literally thousands of miles, connecting with birds, trees, clouds, and other life forms, in search of truth. It is during meditative walking that my head clears of its endless chatter, my senses sharpen, and I am most open to receiving the direction I seek. When I walk, I acknowledge that I am one with the Universe. I connect in a conscious way to the blending of my personal energies with the energies of the Divine in All. I permit fears, worries, and regret to be taken from me, and I make the intention to be open to receiving a full measure of the goodness of life. As I receive, I send unconditional love to all that has been created. It is often following these short moments of conscious connectedness with my own need for releasing difficult emotions, and for giving and receiving love, that I feel most in tune with and in awe of all that surrounds me. And it is most often during these moments of standing in awe, with a mind clear of chatter and fear, that I strongly sense the guidance and direction that the spiritual world offers.

So, although it was with great awe, it was without surprise that on that morning in Bali, when I focused on sending healing energy to my mother, I was instantly shown an answer. It was not the one I expected, yet the one I recognized to be of great truth. I was being encouraged not to hold my mother in captivity. I was being asked to set her free.

Pondering this experience and the lessons it taught, I recognized that much of my professional work provided similar teachings. In each situation I worked to help men and women find their inner freedom. The more I pondered the similarities, the more I acknowledged that my recent work with traumatized women who were incarcerated in our federal prisons was not dissimilar from my previous work with older persons who felt trapped by institutionalization. In each of these circumstances it was not so much the lack of freedom that caused the intense feelings of entrapment; it was more the imprisonment of their spirits. When the spirit feels trapped, the soul's energy wanes. The source of the soul's entrapment matters little.

Bondage of the human spirit occurs in numerous situations. It happens not only within our prisons and long-term care facilities, but also in daycare settings and schools; it happens in our workplaces, our churches, and our homes.

The human spirit has many needs. These include the need to express who we really are, the need to use our talents and creative abilities to their fullest potential, the need to trust and hope, the need to be able to give and receive love, the need to feel a sense of belonging, and the need to feel that we matter and that we make a difference.[1,2,3] When we are in circumstances in which the needs of our spirit cannot be met, our souls cringe. Entrapment of our spirit happens any time we dare not color outside the lines of the particular picture that has been designed for us rather than by us.

Reflecting on the many ways in which our individual and collective souls are held hostage often reminds me of the biblical story of the oppression of the descendants of Jacob.[4] In order to set the Children of Israel free, Moses needed to persuade the Pharaoh that the Israelites were no longer to be used as Egyptian slaves. He began his negotiations using ideas and strategies established within the then-prevalent wisdom, but he soon found it necessary to step outside the reality with which he and the Egyptians were familiar.

To do what was asked of him, it was essential that Moses recognize the presence of the Divine, acknowledge the power of the Divine, and rely on Divine intervention. Moses was compelled to expand his consciousness in ways most of us could only begin to imagine. He was asked to step out in courage, to risk, and to trust that he would be guided as he did so. Moses was asked to shift his own thinking and beliefs, and the thinking and beliefs of those around him. He was asked to transform the reality that he was familiar with by using the supports and interventions offered from another reality. His major task was to "ground" in his third-dimensional world the interventions provided by the spiritual worlds.

Today, in ever-increasing numbers, people from varying walks of life are recognizing a great need for their own personal exodus to freedom. Feeling captive in both their personal and professional lives, and noting the bondage of others, many are searching for ways to transform the servitude mentality so prevalent within their current way of being. Many leaders already acknowledge, as did the philosophers before them, that problems created within one paradigm cannot be solved with solutions generated from within that same paradigm.[5] Recognizing the need for change, they are calling for a new way of viewing reality and a new way of operating in the world. These leaders are asking those who follow to be creative, to take risks, and to think and act outside the box—the box created by a worldview that for the past decades has dominated our culture, a worldview that tends to see only physicality, and generally denies the spirituality of human beings.

Those who have accepted the challenge recognize, as ancient peoples did and as many Indigenous peoples of today do, that we do indeed live in parallel realities. Carl Jung, the famed theorist and leader in modern methods of helping, noted that even in our times the farther we get from countries that are influenced by Western thought, the more people still live in an enchanted world, making little distinction between the sacred and the secular, between the physical and the spiritual realities.[6,7]

Jung's words resounded each day during my visit and study in Bali. Reminders of the gods and the spiritual life of the people were everywhere. Every field was dotted with shrines and temples. The entry to every major intersection, bridge, or irrigation channel had a shrine. Most homes held not one, but several temples. At sunrise I witnessed the priestesses blessing food and flower offerings for placement in home and business shrines as gifts to the gods and in supplication for blessings. The shrines and temples were sculptured interpretations of the Balinese form of Hinduism, of their representation of the afterworld, and of their view of the relationships between the gods and this reality.

Nowhere was the overlap between the coexistence of the spiritual world and this dimension more evident than in the elaborate death rituals and cremation ceremonies that have, over the centuries, changed very little.[8] In the death ritual, loved ones mingle around the deceased body prior to the procession to the place of outdoor and open cremation. Some pour water from tiny clay cups, and others scatter marigolds and other types of flowers on the face and torso. Others bathe the body in sacred ritualistic fashion.

The Balinese believe that death is a phase in a circular pattern of reincarnation. Every ritual is symbolic of this belief and of their belief in the reality of the spiritual worlds. The water and bathing are symbolic of spiritual cleansing; the flowers symbolize something new that is coming into being. The various flowers communicate a particular spiritual message to the deceased.[9] Marigolds are a metaphor for the soul itself and are used in death rituals in a number of cultures as a reminder to the soul of its Divine light and brightness and, because of this divinity, of its continued existence.

The procession itself is a vibrant pandemonium. An orchestra, composed of dozens of sets of gongs and drums, clangs in a disharmonic frenzy. The purpose is to scare away evil spirits. The body of the deceased is placed on a two-story palanquin, a towering pagoda-like portable bier mounted on a dozen giant bamboo poles. The bier is carried on the shoulders of 20 to 30 men. From the front of the palanquin is stretched a white rope—white to remind the soul of its spiritual essence. Women hold the rope in a ceremonial gesture of leading the funeral cortege to the place of cremation. The men carrying the palanquin frequently break into furious running spins, swirling the entire apparatus in wide circles. This is done to confuse any pursuing evil spirits to ensure that the soul of the deceased cannot be followed and to prevent the evil spirits from retracing the funeral procession and haunting the village.

An eight-foot-high black and white paper bull is mounted on a 12- to 15-foot bamboo platform. The bull represents Nandi, the vehicle ridden by the god Shiva, one of the greatest gods in Hindu cosmology. Shiva is a complex deity seen as a destroyer and a restorer, both as the god of death and the god of rebirth.[10, 11] The bull, hoisted on the shoulders of men, moves in procession just in front of the palanquin, which carries the body of the deceased. When the procession arrives at the place of cremation, the body of the deceased is inserted into a trapdoor in the bull. The bull of Shiva becomes the departed soul's vehicle for the journey to the afterlife.[12]

The symbolism surrounding this death ritual and cremation ceremony is a powerful reminder that in cultures such as this, people exist in a dual world, in a reality that sees little distinction between the world of spirit and this dimension. In a reality rich with symbolism and ritual, the human soul is nourished even in times of hardship. In cultures such as Bali, people live with a clear recognition of their soul's purpose, and they are acutely aware of the mirror reflections between this reality and the world of spirit.

In sharp contrast to the Balinese reality is the lived reality of many in the Western world. Although many in our culture are in great need of the guidance, protection, and nurturing that should be accessible to them during difficult life experiences, most of our methods of helping no longer contain practices, activities, rituals, and ceremonies that focus on the soul's journey, on the primordial battle between good and evil, and on our need as human beings for spiritual guidance and protection. Nor do our methods of helping provide ways for human beings to establish, maintain, and strengthen their coexistence with the spirit world.[13] Even our churches lack the ability to meet these needs. In *Dreamquest*, Morton Kelsey noted, "Few of our churches are providing the symbolic food human beings need for survival. Contemporary men and women are not adequately nourished on a diet of reason, logic and matter alone."[14]

In many parts of the world the symbolic food of glorious music, song, chant, color, art and art forms, dance, and ceremony rich and alive in participation and ritual has been downplayed in recent decades. These experiences once dominated religious practices. Experiences rich in symbolism create an opportunity for personal interpretation at an individual soul level. The extinguishing of symbol has, I believe, shifted the goal of religion from an individual soulful understanding of the sacred and the Divine in one's own life to a collective belief of the Divine messages. These messages are then interpreted and relayed by an appointed representative of the Divine. With few exceptions, the relaying of the interpretations at the collective level, along with the dogmas, creeds, and beliefs, are presented in oral language forms with little ritual or ceremony.

Soul does not easily comprehend oral language; its language is symbolic. Ancient and Indigenous teachings acknowledge that to address the soul, you must speak soul's language. Soul starves on a diet of words. Words are the brain's left-hemisphere food. The brain's left hemisphere responds to verbal and written language and is associated with our masculine energies, our mental abilities, our cognitive minds, and our cognitive capabilities. Left brain activity facilitates order and direction. It helps move our physical lives forward in a structured and constructive way.

Right-hemisphere brain activity is associated with our feminine energies, with our creativity and our nurturing capabilities. Right brain functioning is more closely associated with our feeling states, our emotions, and with things of the heart than with concerns and issues of the physical body and the mind. Sound, light, and other vibrations in the forms of energy work, music, drumming, dance and song, and laughter are more easily interpreted by the right than by the left brain. Symbols that appear in dreams, art, and imagery are also more readily interpreted by the brain's right hemisphere, as are ceremony and sacred ritual.

Oral language is bound by culture and perhaps limited to one lifetime. Soul does not recognize such limitations; its language is broader, more expansive. The language of soul transcends time and space. Words can be easily misconstrued; their meanings change over time and are interpreted according to the accompanying nonverbal inflections sent from the giver of the message. The interpretation of verbal language also depends upon the feeling state and perception of the receiver of the message. Symbolic language carries a deeper truth—truth not altered by mood or circumstance. Symbol, compared with words, is undoubtedly a more powerful and lasting way of putting us in touch with our greatest strengths and our deepest fears. This, of course, is essential to our spiritual evolution.

In ever-increasing numbers, therapeutic helpers from various disciplines are seeking ways to more adequately address the soul concerns of those they walk beside. Although many helpers have acknowledged that we receive dream messages in symbol form and many therapists have become interested in assisting those with whom they work in understanding the dream messages being offered, many do not recognize that our souls use numerous other forms of symbolic expression, always with the goal of providing hope and direction for forward movement along our paths of life.

Through guided imagery, our souls present symbolic messages to us, as well as through each of our art expressions, including doodling. The symbols reflected during these daytime experiences can provide powerful messages if we but take the time to reflect on the symbolic meaning being conveyed from the very core of our being, our soul.

Each time I enter a meditative state or perform a ritual or a ceremony, my everyday third-dimensional reality blends with the realms of the spiritual. I have learned that the more I tune into the language of soul, the more easily and more quickly I can access and work within the realms of spirit.

My first awareness of how easily these realities blend occurred during one of those supernatural in-between times, when the indigo curtain of evening was rapidly descending on the performance of yet another day. My dog Buddy and I had lingered longer than usual. The magic of the season, its colors and fragrances, were too delectable to turn from easily. The scent of overripe cranberries, wafting from a nearby grove, prompted memories of Thanksgiving. The tartness of those savory wild berries had enhanced the festive bird during many celebration times in my youth. Taste and smell memories of cranberry jelly spread thickly on warm homemade buns stimulated my gastric juices, reminding me that lunch had been hours ago.

Movement on the path ahead, where no movement should be, drew me from my reverie and from its source. Although the dimness of the twilight made it impossible for me to determine the circumstances, I realized that something black and white was struggling in a frantic effort to free itself from some entanglement. Inner twinges, not of fear but of urgency, jostled me forward. The nylon webbing from a once-round bale of straw had imprisoned a young magpie.

Sensing my approach, the frantic bird escalated its attempts to gain freedom, only to entangle itself even further in the mass of green fibers. Kneeling, I examined the fragile wings, legs, and claws. Witnessing this helpless creature and wondering whether I could be of any real assistance reminded me of a favorite childhood story. I remembered when Ken Mac-Glocklin had found his beloved horse Flicka[15] entrapped in barbed fence wire. He wished he had obeyed his father's bidding to always carry wire cutters when he was out on the open range. How I wished for wire cutters, for scissors, for anything sharp or knife-like. I noted with gratefulness that, although I did not have any such object, I did have gloves. They would not be of help in removing the webbing, but they would certainly protect my hands from the magpie's beak and claws.

As a child, when I helped my father relocate the mature hens to make room for new chicks, he would encourage me to cover their eyes as I carried them from one pen to another. I recalled how this had often put them in a sleep-like state. Trusting that if this procedure had worked for the hens, it just might work now, I reached with a glove-covered hand and secured the head of the bird. It was then but a simple maneuver to slide the other glove over the magpie, hooding its eyes. Whispering, I assured the frightened creature I would do all I could to free it from its prison. The reassurance and the glove-hood trick worked their magic! In seconds the frantic bird calmed, and although I could no longer see its face or eyes, its stillness and lack of movement indicated that the procedure had produced a sedating effect.

There was much to do and time was of the essence. I needed to take full advantage of the remaining light, for whereas at dusk this task was going to be difficult at best, in darkness it would be impossible.

As I feverishly set to work, it became obvious that, in its struggle to free itself, the young bird had become more entrapped with each movement. Its razor-like claws had badly frayed the twine, causing its legs to be tightly bound in a gnarled mass of twisted fibers. Methodically, I unraveled the web, one frayed thread at a time. The last flush of lavender was barely visible along the western horizon when the final ragged string dropped from the young magpie's right claw.

For the first time since I had discovered this captive, I remembered Buddy. He was a hunting dog. Why had he not paid attention to what was unfolding in this straw pile? The dim light, his failing eyesight, and his chance to linger in the gopher mound had certainly been in the bird's favor. Yet now, and as though my thoughts had aroused his curiosity, he appeared. His approach quickly brought the dazed bird to full alert. What if its wings, its legs were broken? What if it could not fly? I had been so intent on the task at hand, so focused on freeing the magpie from its captivity, that I had not paused to wonder about the effects that the tight bindings and its own struggles might have had. Recognizing that magpies need to fly to stay alive, I questioned whether I had spent all this time freeing a magpie that could not survive.

My doubts were short lived. Free from the glove and its bindings, the alarmed bird, wobbling into a hop-like gait, quickly gained enough flying ability to land safely on a nearby fence post. Relieved and satisfied, I turned homeward. I went only a few steps when the young magpie circled above me three or four times before flying off into the darkness. I knew I had been given a message of gratefulness.

I am a dream therapist and have studied symbolism and its sources. It was not, however, until I was relating this story to a colleague and she questioned the significance of the event that I began to ponder the possibility that the experience might contain a symbolic message for my life.

Magpies are believed to be symbolic of abundance; they are always around when there is a generous supply of food. I was going through some difficult times in those days. I had recently left a well-paying position, intent on living my life in ways more consistent with my own soul's growth and therefore with my real purpose in life. Contracts were slow in manifesting, and reimbursement for work completed was even slower in arriving. Yet three (the number of magic) days after freeing the magpie, I received payment for three overdue accounts. I had taken the time to unbind a magpie, a symbol of plenty. Was this indeed a metaphor? Was the universe trying to tell me that it was up to me to free the flow of abundance?

The experience also caused me to ponder the meaning of black and white, the colors of the magpie. Was it time to release my views of a black and white reality? Was it time to recognize my darkness—the fears that fused me tightly to a third-dimension reality—and to accept myself as light, as a spiritual being, and, in so doing, to acknowledge my place in parallel worlds?

I have noted that when we begin in earnest to pay attention to the messages being conveyed from the parallel universe, we are often surprised at how many images already surround us. Seeing such images with new eyes can be powerfully affirming and validating of our spiritual unfolding.

The name of my company is *Taking Flight International Corporation*. My company's renaming followed a dream in which I saw the logo I now use. The bird-like image initially appeared in the dream state and reappeared shortly after in a meditation and again later as I gazed into the early morning sun. Although I knew that the image was giving my company a new name and accompanying logo, I was also aware that there was more to understand about the image and experiences that were begging for examination and integration into my life.

You might also wish to reflect similarly. Is there more that you may need to become aware of regarding any of your recent activities? Can you integrate more completely the spiritual aspects of those experiences into your life and your life's work? Pay particular attention to any situations that might perhaps be categorized as paranormal. Recall the last time you shared such an experience—one you would describe as spiritual or supernatural. What was the basis for your choice of person to confide in, the person you trusted enough to comfortably relate the experience to? Did you use a testing statement? Did you preface the information with a comment such as "You will never believe this, but…" or "This is really weird, but…?"

How comfortable were you in relating your spiritual experience? Did you leave parts out to soften the load? I notice a tremendous difference in comfort levels among various cultures regarding the sharing of experiences considered to be sacred. Many Caucasians become tense and have considerable difficulty even saying words such as *spirituality* and *healing*, whereas these words are part of the normal parlance for peoples from cultures less influenced by Western thought and beliefs. There appears to be a general lack of trust among Caucasians in this regard, and I often wonder about its source. Does it flow from educational systems, political systems, and religious systems, or from previous times, perhaps times of long ago, when it was unsafe to be associated with anyone or anything related to notions of healing and spirituality for fear of torture or being labeled *witch*.

I believe that the testing statements used prior to relating a sacred experience help to ensure that the information about to be shared will be heard at the level at which it was experienced and that both the content and the speaker will be safe with the listener.

I am also aware that during my own journey of healing following the death of my son, I was catapulted inward, there to rediscover my spiritual essence. During those dark days I found no one with whom I could safely share my expanded awareness. In my professional life I now walk beside others who are deeply wounded, and because of my own soul pain and soul healing, I recognize their journey as a soul walk. I listen intently to their spiritual struggles and their soul's awakening and remembering. I know of the great need to honor their knowing, for I hear and read daily of the experiences of others who likewise feel abandoned when their spiritual path is not consistent with the paths designed by the dominant and well-entrenched models of our day.[16, 17, 18]

At this point in life my mission, and therefore my purpose for writing this book, is to encourage and support others as they too become more attentive to soul concerns. I am keenly aware that once soul concerns have been identified, it is essential to offer interventions that are soulful. For me, this means listening to soul pain and then responding at a soul level. To respond at a soul level it is essential that I recognize the depth from which symbols and other soul images surface and know the meaning behind some of the symbols being expressed. It is from this place of recognition and understanding that I can offer empowering guidance. Such a process not only facilitates the soul healing of those I walk beside, but has also expanded, beyond my wildest dreams, the growth of my own soul.

---

# CHAPTER 2

# MOVING BEYOND FEAR

*Come to the edge, he said.*
*They said: We are afraid.*
*Come to the edge, he said.*
*They came.*
*He pushed them… and they flew.*

Christopher Logue dedicated to Guillaume Apollinaire

Reawakening to the totality of our spiritual essence and remembering that during our Earth walk we place one foot in this dimension while the other remains in the world of spirit is, I believe, an important step in the advancement of our abilities to meet in a truly soulful way our own healing needs and the healing needs of those we walk beside. This awareness, in and of itself, seems to create opportunities that invite us to strengthen our abilities to receive the incredible support and healing available in and from higher dimensions. Awareness of who we are and what we are capable of being and doing is directly related to how blocked with fear or how clear of fear we are, for our greatest fear is what we are capable of becoming should we fully embrace our Divine potential. As Marianne Williamson so aptly noted: It is not our weakness, but our greatness, that we fear most.[1] It is not our humanness, but our Godness; it is not our inabilities, but our great potential from which we run. The fears of claiming our true identity and the gifts that flow to us when we embrace that identity surface from a very real source. These fears have been laid down over the centuries and have been deeply ingrained in our individual and collective consciousness.

Every cell in our body holds memory. Each cell is infused with memories of experiences from this lifetime as well as memories of experiences from former lifetimes. Many of us carry deep cellular information that links torture and death with participation in ceremonies that honor our Oneness.

In Europe during the Dark Ages, people suffered incredible injustice and pain at the hands of those who desired to separate the individual from their direct connection to the Divine. This reign of terror was so intense and so severe that, at its end, the masses were scourged of any desire to connect in any direct way with the spirit world. Stripped of personal power at their core, at their souls' level, terrorized individuals were left with little alternative but to rely on the priests to design their worship and mediate on their behalf with a god. This god was described and venerated in ways very different from the Creator they knew and from the celebrations and ceremonies they had designed and participated in previously.[2]

My experiences in dream and regression therapies have convinced me that the pervasive disbelief regarding individuals' ability to heal or to receive a treatment in which the healing is complete and lasting, as well as the underlying fears of those who have healing abilities, is related to the stored memories of those torturous times. Many of us carry such memories of times when it was extremely unsafe to associate with, or even speak to someone, especially a woman, who might be considered a midwife, a healer, a heretic, or a pagan. Such associations were causes enough for torture and death, not only for the associates themselves, but for their families and kin as well. I now also understand that the insecurities and lack of willingness to acknowledge the call to embrace healing gifts that most healers experience as they begin to recognize their abilities and life's purpose are directly related to underlying feelings of dread that surface from these subconscious memories.

Many healers are currently reawakening to their gifts and the abilities that they had developed in previous incarnations. As this awareness surfaces and excitement about their potential grows, many begin to eagerly pursue numerous and various avenues in hopes of reacquainting themselves with this ancient knowing. As they step forth ready to serve in the promotion of healing and spiritual growth, most are astounded to recognize that not everyone on this planet is committed to healing and wholeness; that, in fact, many spend considerable time blocking exactly that from taking place.

As the fears and the challenges surface, aspiring healers often return to dormancy. The challenges that surface reawaken the cellular memories of pain inflicted as a result of being labeled *witch* when they had previously dared to explore their spirituality and use their spiritual gifts. This fear holds many potential healers in captivity. Fear keeps them from fulfilling their life's purpose. Fear blocks their soul's growth. This same fear subsequently blocks what each healer should be offering humanity and therefore also blocks the collective soul's growth. And although a healer may consciously choose to ignore his or her healing gifts and attempt to keep them hidden behind these mounds of fear, the nagging from deep within will not be silenced.

The reason for each incarnation is to advance as a spiritual being. To do so, our soul must express itself using its unique gifts and abilities. When this expression is not allowed to unfold, our souls' growth does not advance. Our souls scream for this recognition. The messages are presented in numerous forms: They appear in our dream life; our artwork and doodles; the songs we listen to, sing, and hum; the colors we choose to decorate with; and even the events that seem synchronistic in our lives. All are soul messages mirroring to us that which we have committed to do and become in this lifetime.

My own body carried much cellular memory of past experiences in which I had been tortured for using my healing gifts and for speaking the truth about the relationship between healing and spirituality. Several years ago I journeyed in pilgrimage to the Languedoc village of Rennes-le-Chateau in the South of France, searching for truth about the Black Madonna and the Jesus mysteries relating to his marriage to Mary Magdalene, their child Sarah, their royal blood line, and the Cathars, Knights Templar, and Priory of Sion.[3, 4, 5, 6, 7, 8] While standing on the remains of a once ornate archway overlooking the fertile Languedoc valley, I was momentarily transported to a previous time. For one instant on that calm day in July 2001, my short, blond hair was instead long and dark. Whipped by fierce winds, my tangled curls created a look of wildness, affirming, I am sure, the justification for my conviction and torture. Hands and feet bound at my back to a mast-like structure, I was suffocating in a stanching smoke that rose from the heat and flames ravaging my own flesh. In my agony I witnessed two jeering women drawing straws to determine future ownership of my belongings.

A similar vision-like-experience occurred in my dream state while I was in Glastonbury, England. This time, bound in spread-eagle fashion, I was suspended beneath a gigantic wooden wheel that two hooded figures were rotating. Each turn of the wheel tore at my body, pulling limbs from torso. For only a second, but with great clarity, I reheard the sneers of my captors and reexperienced the terror and excruciating pain of having my right hip torn from its socket.

In the past, soul-level remembrances of those terrorizing experiences had triggered physical responses in my body. These responses created a strong resistance against my ever again stepping forth to speak of spiritual truths. My body deeply feared similar outcomes. Prior to any degree of acknowledgement of stored memories and their relationship to my bodily responses, I began to recognize a connection between the word *betrayal*, and/or any action on the part of another that could be conceived as betrayal or as an attempt to keep me silent, and the experiences of pain and numbness in my right hip and down my right leg.

My first awareness of such a connection occurred immediately upon my discovery that my creative and therefore soulful work had been plagiarized. I had poured great amounts of effort and personal resources in terms of time, education, research and experience, and physical, mental, emotional, and soul energy into that work, and I had been cut from the team. The two remaining team members had claimed the entire project. In that instance the numbness in my physical body appeared prior to my conscious ability to acknowledge what had actually taken place. The physical response was so intense that I had great difficulty making my way to a nearby treed area, the seclusion of which I desperately needed. The uncontrollable tears and the wailing that poured from me that afternoon, on into the evening and night and throughout most of the next day, erupted from a source and a depth that I did not know existed within me.

Because of the work in which I am now engaged, I hear the life narratives of others. On occasion I hear of experiences when they too have released sorrow stored at a similar depth. I now acknowledge that tears that flow with such intensity pour forth from wells of the remote past and are in some way related to experiences in another lifetime that the soul is committed to setting right in this lifetime. And yet it is the very fear created in the previous incarnation that acts as a barricade, blocking the soul's advancement.

My life experiences and my work with others have taught me two steps that are essential to being able to break through these barricades of fear. Awareness is the first step in changing any behavior. In *Journey to the Sacred: Mending a Fractured Soul*[9] I disclosed the crisis in my personal-beliefs and my intense struggles with the fear-based and disempowering religious teachings that I had been taught as a child. My need to make sense of and come to terms with the death of my son forced me into vicious combat with beliefs and doctrine that I had previously taken as fact, as do the majority of Christians. My intense desire to know truth forced me to leave few stones unturned. To my horror, I discovered that much of what I practiced and believed had been introduced into Christianity as a way of controlling the masses and placing power in the hands of a few. It plagued me to unearth information about the similarities between the Jesus stories and those of numerous pagan gods. I learned about the Council of Nicaea in 325 CE and that the divinity of Jesus had been decided by a vote, and that it was that vote which became the catalyst for the torture and mutilation of heretics (the word *heretic* was coined to refer to those who choose beliefs and practices other than those endorsed by the church.) Shock, denial, and disbelief became constant companions as I scoured the documents for evidence of the introduction of notions such as sin and hellfire into Christian doctrine. The removal of such teachings as reincarnation was a way of infusing fear and an attempt to maintain church control. My skills as a researcher and my need to know the truth to heal my own soul pain eventually forced me to shamefully conclude that a large measure of what I had for so much of my life accepted without question, taught, and even judged others for not believing was not of Divine origin, but was of human orchestration, and often for sinister purposes.

Recognition of the fears and their sources, although not easy, was transforming. Breaking through the fears allowed a gigantic door within me, to creak open.

The more I challenged my fears, the more I recognized, acknowledged, and acted upon the truths garnered from my own knowing and experiences. I began to live and work from a place beyond the restraints of fear-based practices created within paradigms perpetuated by authority figures and powerful institutions that were designed to disempower and control. The more I did so, the more I experienced a direct connection to the Creator and the Divine in All, and the more I was able to slowly and gently reclaim my birthright. This I have come to know as the second step in helping a soul claim freedom. Claiming our birthright is the second phase of transformation.

It took a cosmic shove for me to dig beneath the surface of my deeply entrenched beliefs. It took a cosmic shove to unearth truth. My life's work taught me that this is often the case with others as well. The need to make sense of and find meaning in a difficult life experience is frequently a catalyst that plunges us into the depths of our soul, there to face numerous challenges with long-held beliefs. During such times the unceasing nagging from deep within forces us to examine and reexamine every thought we have, every word we say, every word we hear. Although soul-searching experiences are intensely painful, the benefit of the scrutiny is such that, at the end of our soul's dark night, we know without a doubt what is truth for us. We clearly identify which beliefs we no longer hold. We discern and we recognize the beliefs that are not based upon our own experiences and our souls' knowing, but are instead beliefs into which we have been indoctrinated. We shamefully acknowledge that, because of our unquestioning acceptance, we have contributed to the propagation of beliefs that hold the majority of those who subscribe to these beliefs in positions of powerlessness.

Over the centuries various forms of persecution have taken place not only in Europe, but also in numerous parts of the world. Although they are often endorsed in the name of "God," persecution is always enacted to control and disempower. Persecution is always a means of taking power from individuals and placing it in the hands of a political establishment. Frequently disguised as religious zeal, persecution is always about politics and financial gain. It is never about assisting individuals and the collective on their spiritual journey.

And persecution continues today. It exists in many forms, both overt and covert, in our homes, our institutions, communities, churches, societies, and cultures. We tend to think of persecution in relation to the atrocities inflicted upon the physical body, but persecution of the mind, the emotions, and the spirit also happens in numerous ways and under numerous circumstances. Whenever the status quo is maintained by fear-based rules, persecution is taking place. Whenever individuals and groups are barred from growing in the discovery of their own truth and are coerced into acting contrary to their convictions, persecution is taking place. Whenever we as individuals adhere without question to black and white fear-based beliefs, we submit to the persecution of our own souls. In our subservience we block our souls' ability to advance in order to attain the knowing of our true identity and destiny.

A number of years ago I guided a weeklong learning experience for counselors who, upon completion of their program, would be qualified to assist young people in moving beyond a life of drug and alcohol addiction. My role was to facilitate learning experiences that could allow these future helpers to grow personally and professionally so as to be able to respond to others more from a place of their own healing and wholeness than from a place of their own past hurts and unhealed wounds. Every aspect of this learning center had been architecturally designed to support such a healing journey. The large windows encircling the circumference of the classroom helped to create a milieu of unbroken connection with the natural environment and gave the nonverbal message that in our journey to wholeness, we must come to acknowledge and honor the Creative Force that binds all as one.

On the second afternoon of my time with the group, our work was interrupted by a sickening thud. A woodpecker had flown into the glass and fallen to the ground. Immediately, a number of participants ran through the open doorway to examine the effects on the bird. It is difficult to describe the paralyzing terror that raged through the classroom as these participants received the news that the woodpecker had died. The oldest member of the group affirmed that this bird had been a sign from the spirit world and that its death was an announcement that someone in the group would receive bad news—most probably news about death. He proclaimed that the bird must be burned and the area cleansed. The participants responded by giving him tobacco to use as a prayer offering in exchange for their protection and the protection of their loved ones and to supplement the burning of the bird. Regardless of the rituals performed, regardless of the prayers and the offerings, regardless of the intervention techniques provided, many in the group remained in an emotional paralysis that significantly altered both their attention and their retention abilities.

Because one of our learning objectives was to examine the relationships among beliefs, thinking, attitudes, and behaviors, I decided to capitalize upon the teaching opportunity in this event. And because the participants were about to move into a counseling role, I believed that it would be valuable for them to recognize the relationships between their fears and their belief systems and to have them acknowledge circumstances that trigger their fears. I hoped that these participants would recognize the ways in which they were responding, not from their soul's knowing, but from fear.

I informed them of my belief that there are really only two fundamental emotions—love and fear—and that all other emotions stem from these two. Fear is separation; love is connection. Fear is exclusion; love is inclusion. Love recognizes the Divine in All; fear rejects this Oneness.

I told the students that their souls knew the absolute truth about this situation as well as about each and every situation they faced. I described how fear thoughts surface from ego and are based upon past learning and past experiences, in both this lifetime and previous incarnations.

I asked the group participants to ponder whether their first thought, their souls' thought, had been awareness that a bird can be a messenger from the spirit world. I asked them to acknowledge whether they had a choice in how they responded to that first thought. I asked that they identify whether their next thoughts had been based in love or formulated in fear.

We spent considerable time that afternoon discussing fear and how fears are triggered. Many group members concluded that it is generally not the event that makes us respond in certain ways, but rather the fear-based emotion attached to the event that triggers the response.

The learning goal was to have these participants recognize that they were likely responding to the bird's hitting the window in much the same way as they had learned in childhood to respond to such an event. I encouraged them to examine how they had learned as children to experience fear by modeling the fear being expressed by the "powerful others." I asked them to examine how this fear that had been instilled during their childhood was continually being reinforced by the powerful others who surrounded them today.

Although most of us have entered this lifetime carrying fears infused from past incarnations, we each receive indoctrination into our present belief system during our formative years. As young children we have little ability for rational thought; we respond emotionally to life circumstances. As young children we pick up the emotional state of those around us, and these emotions are infused into every cell of our being. We learn the appropriate and inappropriate emotions and emotional responses that correspond with the events and circumstance that surround us. We also learn to model the physical reactions that are associated with each emotional response. The degree to which we are impacted is directly related to the intensity of the emotional and physical responses expressed by those who are most powerful in our eyes.

Until we examine the origin of these deeply stored emotions, each time we witness or experience a similar event, we respond emotionally and physically in an almost identical way to the way that we learned initially. Each time that we respond in an emotional way to an event, the event triggers our stored emotion and emotional response. And when these responses are continually reinforced and rewarded by the powerful others around us, the emotion and emotional responses we previously attached to the event become, in our view, the only right and true way of viewing and responding to such an event.

Think for a moment of the horrendous actions against women around the world that flow from belief systems and result from fear-based emotional responses. Ponder the recent news story of the mother who killed a daughter who had been impregnated through rape. In the mother's own words, the daughter had to die so that her family could "save face" in their community. This mother's early indoctrination into these beliefs and their reinforcement throughout her life and the expectations of those from within the paradigm to which she belongs deemed her responses to be correct and appropriate ways for her to react; those not immersed in that belief system deemed her actions horrendous.

Back in the classroom, after viewing the dead bird, some group participants became pale and clammy. Some felt faint. Others saw images of loved ones passing. Yet the participants who had not been raised within that belief system had little emotional response to the event. Some viewed the entire situation and the topic of omens and superstitious beliefs (which became a part of that day's discussions) as figments of the imagination and equated imagination with unreality. Nothing, however, could be farther from the truth. The imagination is the power of the mind to create and work with images. Imagination is a powerful tool that opens doors to our own subconscious and to other realms. Here, visions and even prophecies manifest. If we move into these realities seeking fear, we will discover fear. If we move into these realities in search of peace and abundance, that will be our find. In these realities we can receive torture or we can receive assistance in healing and in discovering forgotten knowledge. Our choice is to decide how we will use this gift. Our mind is a powerful tool. We are told we use only 10% of its capacity. Yet even though we use so little of our potential, we create within our minds the reality that manifests for us in the exterior worlds. We create our heavens and we create our hells. What will we do when we become capable of using greater capacities of the brainpower with which we have been endowed?

That day I invited the participants in the counseling group to examine the choices they were making. I asked them to reframe the experience and to examine the event using rational thought rather than fear-based emotion. Did, for example, the woodpecker hit the window because it was attracted by the reflection and saw this as another piece of the great outdoors? I invited them to stay with their initial beliefs but encouraged them to examine the origin of those beliefs and to thereby gain advanced knowledge of the omen and the attached symbolism.

As noted previously, the belief that birds are messengers from the spirit world, which has been a part of the teachings of many ancient societies, still lingers in many cultures. Although the wisdom contained within these traditional teachings is being reawakened,[10] many do not understand the differences between the symbolisms contained within an omen, and superstition. Superstition is fear based whereas an omen is based in knowledge of the natural environment. The reading of an omen flows from having knowledge of the environment, the animals, and other natural elements. Omens border upon a recognition of the relationship between events in nature and circumstances in our lives.

A friend who grew up in Guatemala spoke of an incident in his childhood that reinforced his belief in omens. He recalled that for about a week prior to the major earthquake that took place in his country in 1976, large numbers of ants appeared. Each ant was feverishly engaged in an endeavor to carry either food or young. He recollected the neighborhood conversations about the ants and their obvious relocation activities. He noted that this activity ceased a few days before the earthquake actually occurred and, following the shock and during the cleanup, people remembered this omen. When we know and understand the patterns of nature and the patterns of the insects, animals, and birds that are normally around us, we recognize alterations in their behaviors. We pay attention to the unusual. The difficulty lies perhaps in the inability to define, explain, and apply the omens of nature to our lives.

Superstition, on the other hand, is built upon a lack of understanding of the omen and the significance of the omen. For example, the situation in Guatemala would be an ideal situation from which to create a superstition.

Rather than understanding that the ants were relocating to safety and that the omen was a mirror that reflected the need for human beings to do likewise, those in positions of recognized power could easily convince those readily swayed by fear to view any future groups of ants as harbingers of death.

Superstitions flow from irrational fears and frequently involve actions to avoid bad luck. Superstition, like knowledge of the natural world, is generally passed on verbally through the generations. Superstitions always have elements of control and personal disempowerment. They hold the believer in bondage. When we are in bondage to the power of superstition, we are easily manipulated by those who choose to keep us in positions of powerlessness. An omen, in contrast, is used to assist individuals in recognizing their personal power and connecting with the Divine Force in the Great All.

The personal and complete connection with the immediate experience of the bird's flying into the window gave the participants in the counseling course a valuable opportunity to come face to face with their own fears, to examine the origin of those fears and the reinforcement of those fears. The students were then able to make a conscious choice either to continue to hold that belief and the associated fears or to reexamine the belief and the original teachings and perhaps reframe the event by seeking other possible explanations. If they chose to stay with their initial belief, which was that the woodpecker's death was a sign from the spirit world that announced impending death, they were asked to consider whether this choice was based in love or fear. Was this view flowing from fear-based emotion received in childhood and therefore from feelings of powerlessness to control the outcome, or was it based upon their souls' knowing that this omen was a gift being given to them and thereby affording them an opportunity to stand in their own power and perhaps change the energy and therefore the outcome?

People hold different perceptions of natural and supernatural events, and their perceptions are colored by their upbringing, including cultural influences. Many cultures hold beliefs that associate death symbols with messengers from the natural world. Some see the owl as a symbol of protection and healing and often associate it with guiding a healer, especially one who works with those who are moving through very dark experiences. People from other cultures, including those from Germany and Mexico, often view the owl (especially one that is hooting) as a harbinger of death. Because of these deeply ingrained beliefs, many are able to relate stories as evidence that what they believe about these associations is true.

My friend from Guatemala recollected that in his country a black butterfly is associated with death. He remembered a day when he was a young man working in a bank when he and his colleagues had witnessed two black butterflies hovering in a corner near the ceiling. One of the butterflies was larger than are many of its kind; the other was a smaller variety. Two days later the bank was robbed and two employees were shot. One of the dead was a man much larger than most in his culture; the other was a man smaller than most in his community.

I asked my friend whether he believed that the black butterflies had been harbingers of the deaths. He thought the butterflies were aspects or reflections of the souls of the individuals who had died. He believed that this was likely true because, at the moment of his mother's death, his sisters had reported seeing a white butterfly fluttering over their mother's chest. He believed that the outcome for the two men might have changed if the employees had believed that they had the power to manifest change and had taken action based upon that belief.

In *Journey to the Sacred* I described a prophetic dream in which I saw a tragic outcome. Upon awakening from that dream, I knew that I must do everything in my power to change the outcome I had witnessed. I learned in that instance and in many others since that we as human beings have tremendous power to facilitate change. I believe that our Creator has bequeathed to human beings the ability to change the course that energy takes. In the dream that I described in my previous book, I knew that my prayers and my faith in my abilities to manifest change had altered the course of the outcome foretold in the dream.[11]

I shared that dream, my experiences about changing the prophetic outcome and the personal knowing that had resulted from the experiences with the counseling-group participants. I invited them to ponder whether, if the woodpecker had indeed been a harbinger of death, it was possible that they were being offered an opportunity to use their own divine powers and thus alter the forecasted outcome. I also asked them to consider other possible meanings for the symbolism related to the death of the woodpecker.

Having knowledge of symbols and symbolism helps us to look for, interpret, and apply the parallel meanings of the omens that appear in our lives. Knowledge helps us to understand the true messages mirrored from the spirit world rather than blindly accepting the teachings that have been charged with fear to control those who lack this knowledge.

Symbols in omens are similar to symbols in dreams and art forms. Although we can and do have premonition dreams that alert us to our own approaching death or the death of a loved one, the actual physical death is rarely depicted in a dream as actual dying. In many cultures, the forecast of death is more commonly viewed in a dream as though the physical death had already occurred, and it includes seeing the body in a death state. Other common dream symbols that forecast or announce death include a riderless horse, a black horse drawing a carriage, a hearse, or a funeral procession. These symbols more frequently herald actual physical death than do most of the symbols and omens that many have come to associate with death.

Seven months before my mother's death I had two dreams that announced her physical passing. In the first I was picking music to be sung at her funeral. During the subsequent night's dream I witnessed myself and all of Mother's children walking behind her casket as we entered her home-town church. To the best of my knowledge, at the time of these dreams my mother was in perfect physical health, but I knew the dreams were a gift. They were forewarning me that time was running out, and, in doing so, they were offering me an opportunity to complete unfinished emotional and spiritual business. When my mother's time came, she could leave feeling satisfied and at peace with the lifetime we had shared, and I could leave her graveside with few regrets.

In contrast to viewing death symbols that assist us in bringing a satisfactory closure to life or a relationship, dreams in which we see ourselves or a loved one actually die most frequently do not forecast actual physical death, but symbolically reflect a challenge that we must confront. Such dreams often announce the death of one way of being and the rebirth of another.

In *10,000 Dreams Interpreted,* Pamela Ball emphasized that viewing a death in a dream frequently announces the need to adjust our approach to life and to accept that there can be new beginnings if we have courage. The symbol indicates that a change is taking place, and the change is often a shift in awareness. The dream symbol reflects this "rite of passage."[12]

I asked the participants in the counseling group to determine whether it could be possible, for example, that the woodpecker's death was a message from the spirit world that indicated that something, perhaps even their thought patterns, needed to die so that something new could take root.

A few days before my younger daughter's wedding I dreamed she was dying. Had I no knowledge of death symbols, I might have easily dissolved into fear, especially because I know the pain of losing a child. My familiarity with symbols, however—and in this case particularly with death symbols—caused me to pause for a few days, despite the busyness of wedding planning, to reflect on the dream message. I was being guided to note that one way of life was ending, not only for my daughter, who was officially moving into womanhood, but for our entire family. My relationship with her was changing, and her relationship with me and with her father and sister would be forever different.

I was directed by the dream symbols to take time to examine all that had been for us up to this point. I was reminded of what I teach others. It was time to make a choice; it was time to honor how far she had come and rejoice in what we had. It was time to mourn the endings in order to be fully ready to step forward and celebrate the new beginnings.

The participants in the counseling course varied considerably in their abilities and willingness to examine possible explanations other than the ones that they had received as children. Their reactions were similar to the way that most of us respond when our belief systems are challenged. On numerous occasions parents, teachers, and others whom they viewed as all-knowing and powerful had reinforced their beliefs about the death of a woodpecker. The degree of emotional load that they attached to the belief, the degree to which they gave of their personal power to those whom they considered to be all-knowing, and the degree to which they themselves had invested in maintaining that belief were equivalent to the ease or difficulty with which each of them examined other possible ways of viewing the woodpecker's death.

We are all like the participants in this group. We each view the world through a framework carpentered from the religious, cultural, political, and educational systems into which we have been indoctrinated. We all have powerful priests, teachers, elders, parents, and friends who continually reinforce our initial teachings. We invest in these teachings, and our investments strengthen the construction of the framework. The more we invest and the longer we remain in an environment where our beliefs are reinforced, the thicker and stronger are the walls of our framework. The thicker the walls, the greater the difficulty with which we see beyond them, even when there is considerable and ever-mounting evidence to the contrary.[13, 14, 15, 16, 17]

Although our religious, social, cultural, political, and educational systems create our overall framework for viewing the world, each experience that we have as individuals also helps to shape our perceptions of reality. Because we process information according to our own circumstances, each of us, regardless of our culture or religion, sees the world in a somewhat unique manner. Therefore, because of our experiences, we each have tunnel vision. The tunnel can be narrow and limiting, or its circumference can be expansive. Our tunnel vision is our focus, our take on the world. It is created as a process of filtering our life experiences. Each experience, tinted by our beliefs and values garnered from our particular background, is filtered through this tunnel. We examine every word we hear, every action we view, and we attach judgment in the form of a thought. We decide in a split second, and the thought in turn becomes our reality. We decide whether the event is good or bad, right or wrong, black or white, or whether, indeed, the event is gray—neither black nor white, neither good nor bad, but containing elements of both. This is, I believe, what Shakespeare meant when he stated, "Nothing is either good or bad, but thinking makes it so."[18] Shifting our religious, social, cultural, physical, emotional, mental, intellectual, spiritual, or environmental circumstances broaden the circumference of the scope through which we view reality. We are reminded of the necessity to do so; we are promised that the eyes of those who truly see and the ears of those who truly hear are indeed blessed.[19]

Consider how many events take place each day in our world in an effort to maintain, through fear, the status quo of a religious, political, or cultural system. We rarely pause in our active lives to question our responses or the emotions attached. But before we can truly find inner freedom, we must examine our fears. If there is fear attached to any reason for our action or inaction, be it fear of ridicule, fear of rejection, fear of death, or even fear of hell, we are responding from a fear-based belief system.

Because of my work, I hear numerous teachings and beliefs. I listen carefully to recognize attachments. I question," Is this teaching or belief based on love, or is it fear-based?" If fear is attached in any way, I know that this belief is of human origin, and I gently encourage the speaker to ponder his or her need to maintain such a belief.

It takes tremendous determination and often great courage to consciously slow our thoughts and physical responses to an event until we can fully and completely examine our beliefs surrounding that event. It is important also to examine the origins of our beliefs and our usual responses that flow from those beliefs. When we deliberately do so, we are generally able to recognize that we are holding beliefs and responding from the collective emotions that surround us. When we inspect the roots of our beliefs and our responses to them, we often become aware that many of our responses are fear based and that the fear so deeply infused into every cell of our being has little to do with our personal experience of reality or our personal connection to the Divine in All.

Recognizing this truth and beginning to respond from this truth can significantly shift our sense of belonging. We recognize that we are now different and that we can no longer respond in the ways that we previously did. And although we are beginning to feel a greater connection to our own soul and its continuity of being and a keen awareness of how we are actually a part of All, we are, at the same time, experiencing a sense of disconnectedness from the communities where we once experienced kinship. This can leave us searching for ways to fill the void.

This search to fill the void, although it often feels like a lonely and unaccompanied walk, is indeed the journey that we each at some point must make to reclaim our Wholeness, our Oneness. Our journey to Oneness is a journey toward a complete recognition and an embracing of the knowledge that it is our fears that have broken the connection with the One. As we advance in our abilities to live and learn and walk in love, we gather to us the greatest of companions. In their company we are never alone.

# EXPLORING ALTERNATE VIEWS
# OF LIFE AND LIVING

*Problems cannot be solved with the same level of thinking that created them.*

Einstein

Some years ago when I began teaching gerontology, I was given a copy of the *Crabbed Old Woman*,[1] a poem that had apparently been discovered amongst the belongings of a woman who had died after extended residency in a long-term-care facility. The poem's unknown author clearly portrayed her own intense inner pain and cried out for acknowledgement of the individual and collective soul pain of all who are imprisoned within bodies that no longer respond to their commands. The "crabbed old woman" depicts the life of individuals who are at the beck and call of those who provide for their physical needs.[2]

> Communicating for each and every resident in long-term care, the author expressed the longing to be known, to feel a sense of worth and a sense of being valued. She described the soul pain she experienced because of her lack of feeling connected to those around her. No one knew who she really was, or what her life story had been. No one knew what she had contributed to the world, or of her talents and her abilities. No one knew what joys she had experienced during her lifetime, of the sorrows she had overcome, or of the soul pain she still carried. No one knew what healing still needed to happen so that this one soul might feel the integrity that comes from being able to bless one's life feeling a true sense of peace with the One Who Gives Life.[3]

The author was sharing her life-review process and in so doing was delivering her message from a spiritual framework.[4] She begged her caretakers to get in touch with her humanness, to see her personhood, to see the uniqueness of her soul. The poem calls each of us to adjust our perspective, to peek beyond the physical aspects of those around us, to recognize their soul's pain and brokenness, to assist them in reclaiming their soul's wholeness, and to help them once again experience joy.[5]

It appears that those around the crabbed old woman could not hear her desperate cries. It seems that their eyes and ears were attentive only to what was needed to meet their job requirements. Their worldview of resident care likely flowed from that of the organization within which they worked. Because the focus for care appeared to be on addressing physical needs, the staff would place little value on the crabbed old woman's cries of spiritual distress. If they viewed her cries for spiritual comfort as having little worth, there would then be little need to address her soul pain.[6]

The literature suggests that although many health professionals are aware that those in their care have spiritual needs[7,8] and acknowledge that the provision of spiritual care is within the scope of their practice, many describe a lack of educational preparation (and therefore a lack of knowledge about the spiritual dimension). They speak of confusion between religion and spirituality and a hesitancy to introduce the "nonscientific" realm into a science-based practice.[9,10] Even though it has now been several decades since Hubert[11] questioned whether health care professionals recognize a spiritual need and understand their responsibility for providing spiritual care, numerous other women and men in long-term-care facilities could have authored the poem. The story of one such resident, Mirabella, remains indelibly imprinted in my mind and heart.

The nursing team leader had asked me to assess and suggest strategies to alleviate the intense anxiety that Mirabella was feeling. I was a graduate student doing a clinical practicum, studying the mental health concerns of older people who, for whatever reasons, were living their remaining years in an institution.

Mirabella had suffered a global stroke. She had lost the use of her limbs and her ability to speak. A speech therapist had designed a computerized board that was reprogrammed on a regular basis with greetings that pertained to Mirabella's life. A probe was attached to a band around her head. When she wanted to communicate, she could bend her head and touch the probe to a letter board, and the listener could hear the programmed greeting or could wait and read the words and sentences that Mirabella attempted to spell out by using her probe, letter by letter.

It is not difficult to imagine how infrequently the staff was able to take the time to wait patiently and interpret what Mirabella was attempting to write. It is also not hard to envision that most of the time spent on interpreting her messages was focused on meeting her physical needs. It takes less time to communicate in nonverbal forms the need for a drink or the bathroom or the desire to be positioned than it is does to communicate emotional and spiritual distress.

Because my reason for being in that facility was to study mental health concerns in detail and in depth, I spent long periods of time corresponding with Mirabella and hearing of her life—of her successes and of her intense soul pain. I was deeply touched by the humanness of the story that unfolded. She communicated a deep longing to be known. She had graduated as a nurse. As an ambassador's wife, she had traveled extensively and worked internationally. She had lived in an "elegant" home; she had "fine china" and "expensive jewelry." However, there was no evidence in her immediate environment to communicate any part of her life's story. Her room was void of any of these extensions of her personhood. Even her wedding rings had been sent to her son's home for safekeeping.

Through tears, Mirabella laboriously used the probe to communicate her distress because no one knew who she really was. Letter by letter, I learned that she had worn "fine undergarments" that were "quality." Now she wore "diapers."

Her husband had been a faithful companion who had spent each afternoon at her bedside until his death several months previously. She had raised two sons, who rarely visited because they found it "too difficult." When they did visit, they spent most of their time communicating with staff about how to better meet their mother's physical care needs.

After gathering numerous snippets of Mirabella's story, a family and staff meeting was arranged to communicate, not physical care needs, but her emotional and spiritual concerns. Most important, the goal of the gathering was to identify ways to ease her soul pain and emotional distress. I reiterated her narratives and described her perception of her current reality. Through tears and sobs, sons and grandsons suggested ways to enrich Mirabella's life, and we took the suggestions to her. With her delighted approval, a curio cabinet, originally an anniversary gift from her husband was placed in a position in her room where she could easily view it from her bed. A few precious pieces of china, her wedding rings and a selection of her favorite jewelry, her nurse's cap, family photos, and memorabilia from her travels were locked behind the glass doors of this elegant mahogany piece.

Even though the staff had no more time than they previously had to communicate with her, their comments as they focused on her beautiful possessions indicated a broadened understanding of her past history as a nurse, an ambassador's wife, a mother, and a grandmother. The extensions of Mirabella's personhood, as the tokens in her cabinet revealed, stimulated a heightened level of awareness and of subsequent conversation and behavior on the part of all who entered her room. The staff members' comments revealed an increased acknowledgement of the wholeness of the aphasic woman who required others to meet her every need. Through tears of joy during soul-touching follow-up visits, Mirabella communicated that the staff now saw her as a woman of "class." She felt a sense of being known, a sense of importance. She indicated that even though she had to wear protective underwear, the staff now recognized her as a "lady."

Both sons were quick to witness the difference. It had been difficult for them to be with their mother when she was distressed, but they eagerly modeled the staff's heightened positivity and attentiveness. The photos and other memorabilia stimulated remember-when conversations, which in turn reinforced the positive aspects of their lives together and healed the strained ones.

The changes in communication and the reactions of the staff and her family members not only indicated increased sensitivity to the totality of Mirabella's humanness, but also helped her to identify for herself the many threads that had contributed to the fabric of her life. This recognition was immensely valuable in helping Mirabella to view her life as a meaningful whole. And, in the final analysis, she was able to move beyond feelings of despair to the recognition that she had done the best she could. Doing this life review released Mirabella from her soul's anguish. She died four months later, and I believe that she had found peace at life's closure.

The changes in the reactions of others relieved Mirabella's intense loneliness and helped to meet a deep-seated soul need—the spiritual need for connectedness. The spiritual need for human connectedness is described as a longing to be known, to feel that we belong, that we are important, and that our lives have value and significance.[12] Yet how many of our parents, grandparents, neighbors, and friends must pack their entire life into one box and one suitcase when they enter a long-term-care facility? Belongings are extensions of our personhood. We invest much emotional, mental, and spiritual energy into the possessions with which we surround ourselves—the memorabilia we treasure for whatever reason. Although a spiritual goal is to accept that possessions in and of themselves do not bring happiness, it is also necessary to acknowledge that, as in Mirabella's case, our possessions, the items we cherish, and the belongings with which we surround ourselves not only describe us to the world, but also in many ways describe the world to us. These same items frequently hold a history that connects them to a particular life event, often an event that somewhere long ago triggered a turning point. Attention to a treasured item generally stimulates recall of the event, of the joys and the sorrows associated with that turning point, and thereby providing a great opportunity for healing any associated pain and for celebrating life's successes.

Turning points are life events after which things will never again be the same. We experience numerous turning points throughout the course of life and, depending on the degree of associated losses, some turning point events are significantly more difficult to cope with and adjust to. One spring morning early in my career as an educator, a student requested assistance in the management of such a turning-point experience.

Jacob, an older long-term care resident who was usually calm and of a gentle nature, was, on that particular morning, reported to have been physically and verbally abusive with a number of staff members. After a search of the premises, the student and I found Jacob standing near an open window at the far end of the facility. Tears streaming down his face, he was apparently lost in sorrow, hearing the distant rhythmic banter of an auctioneer attempting to get a higher bid for a particular piece of his farming equipment.

His agitated behaviors were clearly a physical response to the stripping away of the frayed fibers that were already barely able to hold together this elderly farmer's life fabric. "For his own good" he had been placed in respite care so that the sale of his life's investment could be conducted without a scene. When I asked what would make the day easier for him, he responded with quivering voice, "I wanna talk to the guys buying my stuff." Neither I nor the student could take him to the auction, but his answer indicated that this was perhaps not his utmost need. His response signaled a deeper request, a desire to be heard—a desire to relate the life narrative that each piece taken to the auctioneer's block would stimulate. Agitation turned easily and gently to calm and gratefulness as he realized that his audience was eager to learn how these parts of metal and steel had helped to fashion his life.

Each piece of equipment held a story, a soul story; each story communicated an aspect that made up the totality of one human being. Each narrative proclaimed his sense of being and belonging, his contributions to the world, and his place in that world.

He was required to leave behind all that had given his life meaning and purpose, all the memorabilia that marked his life's contributions. By recognizing his soul's concerns and responding at a soul level, the caring student was able to soothe the pain in this older gentleman's aching soul. In exchange, she received an incredible gift.

Although she was grateful to have been able to offer the older gentleman meaningful caregiving, the student left his side that morning aware of how much she too had benefited both personally and professionally. In offering her a glimpse of his soul's history, the older gentleman had taught her much about his world and his view of reality. Their soul-to-soul exchange had not only altered her view of what was really important for him, but it had also dramatically changed her view of care and caregiving.

Since the early 1970s, philosophers have reminded us that a worldview is a lens through which we see the world. It is however, not simply a way of interpreting what we see, but that the same information seen through a different lens will actually lead us to see different things. The way we view our reality—what we see as important to pay attention to and also what we do not regard as valuable—flows directly from our own particular view of the world. Our worldview creates a tunnel vision that literally blocks us from seeing certain things. I once read that the Caribbean people were amazed that Columbus and his men had crossed the ocean in such small boats—those used by the explorers to row from their ships to the shore. When the larger vessels anchored in the deeper waters were pointed out, the islanders were unable to see them. Their view of reality did not include water-going vessels larger than canoes, and they could therefore not regard the ships that the explorers described as a possibility. For them, such ships could not exist; their particular view of reality blocked them from seeing what the explorers knew to be true.

The health professionals to whom I referred at the beginning of this chapter who described their practice as scientific and spirituality as nonscientific identified little need to address the spiritual concerns of clients. Those who viewed spirituality as an important aspect of their own life saw a great need to address their clients' spiritual concerns.[13] Professionals who define spirituality in terms of religion tend to believe that ordained clergy or recognized faith group leaders should offer spiritual interventions. Professionals who define spirituality as a concept broader than religion regard their assistance with the spiritual concerns of those within their care as an important responsibility.[14, 15, 16, 17]

How we describe and define what we see as important creates a huge mirror for those around us, one that clearly reflects our views of the world and the paradigm from within which we operate.

In the 14th century during the Black Plague, physicians did not look for or see microbes as causes of infectious diseases. One could argue that this was merely because no lenses existed for microscopes. But because doctors of that day practiced with an astrological worldview, they perceived the cause of disease to be within the stars and the constellations, so they saw no need to devise such an instrument. Paradigms shifted, and today the majority of physicians identify germs as the causative agent of infectious diseases.

From which of these worldviews do we discover the accurate cause of infectious diseases? Interestingly, practitioners from within each paradigm have found evidence to support their beliefs. Those who view the malady as bearing planetary influences locate visible signs to support their diagnoses. Physicians who subscribe to the germ theory detect evidence of microbes as the causes of the disease. These are two distinct worldviews— both bearing evidence in support of their reality, even though one group's reality completely contradicts the other's. Is one right and the other wrong? Is either right? Are both wrong? Is it possible that both worldviews hold elements of truth?

Many older people receiving long-term care display symptoms of psychiatric illness. For centuries, behaviors we now refer to as psychiatric symptoms were believed to be caused by the possession of a dark or evil force or forces. The paradigm shifted, and practitioners began to view aberrant behaviors as manifestations of mental illness and, in support of this worldview, began discovering symptoms to validate their observations of a psychiatric disorder rather than a sign of a spiritual intrusion.

Over the past decades the criteria for identifying psychiatric symptoms and diagnosing and prescribing treatment for psychiatric illnesses have been clearly articulated to those who practice in these arenas. In ever-increasing numbers, however, these very same practitioners are becoming disenchanted with the models and systems into which they have invested so much of their time, energy, and commitment. Many are recognizing the numerous cases that do not neatly fit the criteria for the diagnosis. Practitioners are beginning to concede that the language developed for use within their practice models often does not accurately describe the manifesting symptoms or the patient's experiences. Phenomena, categorized as paranormal, as being outside the box, are being recognized and along with this awareness there is an even greater acknowledgement. When symptoms do not fit the diagnosis, the treatment regime fails to eradicate the symptoms, and the deviant behaviors continue.

The worldview of shamans and other spiritual healers is quite different from that of clinicians of psychiatric medicine. Spiritual healers associate psychiatric problems with a spiritual concern. They identify spiritual intrusions as the major cause of aberrant behaviors. They view spiritual intrusions as the invasion and subsequent habitation of an individual's psychic or soul space by a foreign and undesirable energy or entity. The shaman's and the psychiatrist's worldview are distinct from each other; yet both have well-established processes for identifying causes and removing symptoms. Both have different measures for determining success. For decades neither group has found the need to alter its views or exchange information. In *Entering the Circle*,[18] Olga Kharitidi, a Russian psychiatrist, described her discovery of the ancient secrets of Siberian wisdom. She shared the spiritual knowledge that she received from the shaman and described the application of this knowledge to psychiatric practice. Daring to cross the tightly drawn lines of professional paradigms, Kharitidi found ways to do soul healing. She helped many find their inner freedom.

Others like her, including nursing theorist Martha Rogers,[19] have dared to do similarly. Drawing on her background in physics, Rogers began to ask why the gradual increase in pulse and blood pressure that is often seen with each advancing decade was viewed only as a sign of illness, and she invited her colleagues in the health care professions to explore other possibilities as well. She asked that they begin to shift the paradigm from within which they practiced. She encouraged the exploration of other possible conclusions from the symptoms than those that professionals trained within the illness paradigm had been educated to draw. Following her lead, others began to question whether the increased frequencies noted in the electrical mechanisms of the cardiovascular system during aging indicate not so much wear and tear as ever-increasing energy frequencies and movement.[20]

If we step out of the well-entrenched illness models based upon pure scientism and view aging unconventionally, would we ask different questions during our assessments and accept alternate data as indicators of our diagnoses? Tiptoeing from the well-established worldview and looking in unique ways at the evidence might demand that we determine whether the signs of increased energy frequencies could indicate something other than symptoms of advancing illness and deterioration. Could these increased frequencies also and perhaps more significantly, suggest preparation by the physical body for release of the spirit energy back into the higher frequencies from which it came?

If we were to see things differently, would we then behave differently? If we were to perceive older persons as spiritual beings who were ending their physical experience and their time of learning in this dimension, would we then recognize them as spirits that have gained increased wisdom here? If we viewed human beings from a spiritual rather than a physical perspective, would we acknowledge the enormous soul growth that has taken place for the unique individuals who linger in our nursing homes? If we were to see aging as a time of culmination of spiritual progress, knowing that the older persons before us have come into this lifetime with a unique set of soul lessons to be learned, would we not then more easily acknowledge that, despite outward appearance, these people have advanced in their soul's overall growth and development? Most importantly, would such recognition generate more positive responses to the aged and to their experiences?

Martha Roger's assumptions[21] about human beings stimulated similar dialogue among researchers and scholars with regard to hyperactive children.[22] Her associates began to examine the relationships between hyperactivity and increased energy frequencies. Their endeavors led them to step outside their tunnel vision in seeking other possible explanations for the causes of the symptoms displayed by children labeled as hyperactive. Clinicians were encouraged to question the illness diagnoses and illness labels that had been attached to these children and their behaviors. Was it possible that the children diagnosed as hyperactive were resonating at a higher energy frequency than the rest of humanity? If so, did practitioners desire to slow these children down with drugs, or did they instead wish to find ways to assist these children and their care providers in channeling this energy in creative and productive ways?

Insightful researchers and clinicians began to wonder whether these children, rather than being ill, are perhaps leaders. Are they the Dew-line, the first alert of a more rapid energy frequency that humans on this planet will require? Will all of humanity be required to speed up to this energy frequency to be able to respond to some yet unknown Earth changes?

In their book the *Indigo Children*,[23] Lee Carroll and Jan Tober noted that many of the children labeled ADD (attention deficit disorder) and ADHD (attention deficit hyperactive disorder) demonstrate hyperactive behaviors and suggested that many of these children are highly intelligent and appear to be very developed spiritually. They described the children as *Indigoes*, indicative of the intense color identified in their auras by those who have clairvoyant vision. Indigo is the color most frequently associated with spiritual development. Doreen Virtue, a contributor to the book *Indigo Children*, wrote, "We know that Indigo Children are born wearing their God-given gifts on their sleeves." She described them as naturally born philosophers who ponder the meaning of life and how we might save the planet. Virtue emphasized that these children "are inherently gifted scientists, inventors, and artists. Yet, our society, built upon the old energy, is smothering the gifts of the Indigo Children."[24] She noted that the main objective of the National Foundation for Gifted and Creative Children is to reach out and help these precious children because many gifted children are being destroyed in the educational systems. Many are falsely labeled, and many parents are unaware that their children might be gifted.

Nancy Ann Tappe was among the first to identify and write about the indigo phenomenon. In her book *Understanding Your Life through Color*,[25] she emphasized that all these children ask for are to be respected as children and to be treated as human beings. She encouraged no differentiation between children and adults, but equal respect for all.

Throughout their book Carroll and Tober and their contributing authors reported that these children cannot stand to be disrespected, for they know who they are. They know they are great spirits, and they do best when they are treated as adults. They cannot stand to see others, especially their mothers, either disrespecting themselves or allowing themselves to be disrespected.

These researchers and others like them are telling us that it is time to examine old ways of viewing. Although the entire world has benefited in numerous and various ways from the focus over the past decades on illness and illness care and the good created within that paradigm must be preserved, old explanations are no longer offering plausible descriptions for the new phenomena that are occurring. Many researchers, educators, and practitioners are acknowledging that phenomena occur that do not neatly fit the diagnoses and labels prescribed, and they are beginning to look in earnest for other causes and other solutions.

Centuries ago, in an effort to obtain scientific purism, the paradigm pendulum shifted completely away from the spiritual approach to healing. The pendulum now appears to be gently moving toward a state of balance. This, I believe, is in response to the human cry for care and caring that is more holistic in nature. Seasoned practitioners are recognizing that most things are neither black nor white, but carry elements of both, and more. Some are pushing the borders of their own beliefs systems, moving from dichotomous ways in which they have been taught to think, feel, function, assess, and judge everyone and everything; and a few are courageously encouraging those who follow behind to do likewise.

When we step out of the worldview that sees human beings as physical beings in a constant state of decline and step into the worldview that sees human beings on a spiritual journey, we not only observe differently, but also analyze the observations differently. When we analyze the data differently, we prescribe and recommend differently.

When, for example, we observe older persons and hyperactive children from a spiritual rather than a physical framework, we draw different conclusions and search for alternate approaches to assist them and their families. Of equal importance, when we view data through a different lens, we attach different emotional responses to the findings. If, for example, we conclude that hyperactive children and older persons are in need of restraints in both physical and chemical form, we experience numerous emotions, many of which are much less than positive or helpful for them, their families, and their behaviors. If, on the other hand, we view older persons as now ready to leave this dimension having learned a whole new set of soul-advancing lessons, and if we perceive hyperactive children as bringing to the Earth plane first waves of a higher-level spiritual energy, we behold them as leaders and masters. We treat them with dignity and respect rather than rejection. We feel joy, not dismay, in their presence. We do not hamper their soul's growth; we encourage it. If we perceive hyperactive children and older persons in care as spiritual beings rather than as damaged and dysfunctional human beings, rather than avoiding them we desire to be with them in hopes of learning ways in which we too might increase our spiritual energy vibrations. If we perceive all of our older persons and all of our children as spiritual energy, we do not make them color inside the lines; we learn from them the exhilaration of coloring outside the lines.

For decades, philosophers such as Rogers,[26] Kuhn[27] have reminded us that when we examine the data from a different paradigm, we observe different phenomena. In the poem *My Madonna*, Robert Service[28] portrayed this same message. *My Madonna* describes an artist who painted a woman of the street. Viewing the finished product, an art connoisseur exclaimed "Tis Mary, the Mother of God." The connoisseur's comments flow, not from reality, but from his particular view of what is probable. How often do we each do like-wise?

CHAPTER 4

# EXPANDING DEFINITIONS
# OF THE SPIRITUAL

*A mind stretched to a new idea never resumes its original dimension.*

Oliver Wendell Holmes

Because our descriptions and definitions of reality create a huge mirror, reflecting our views of the world and the paradigm from within which we operate, it is valuable to know as fully as possible what images we are really projecting.

Before you read further, take a few moments and complete the following **art activity** in which you depict your particular understanding of spirituality. To do this activity, you will need a piece of construction paper, some magazines, a pair of scissors, glue, and any other supplies needed to make a collage. As you search through the magazines, continuously ponder, "What is essential in my definition of spirituality?" Then cut and paste pictures that depict all that would be necessary for such a definition. Doing this exercise will not only allow you to determine your definition of spirituality, it will also help you to identify the reflections you are mirroring to the world.

When you have completed the collage, list in your journal each picture. Describe what each picture means to you and why you believe that it is needed in this collage. Journal your immediate response, your first thought. Many spiritual teachers encourage attention to our first thought, which indicates that the first thought is from soul. Soul is always encouraging forward movement along our spiritual journey. Soul thoughts are empowering, always trying to get us to acknowledge our true selves. Our second thought is frequently from ego. Soul's language is always about love; it is never based in fear or separation. That is ego's territory. Ego language comes in the forms of lack—too old, too young, not enough—resources, money, or education: "Who do you think you are?" "What will your family say?" "What will the neighbors say?" Ego language is the language of emotion, not the language of soul. Words such as *guilt, shame,* and *anger* are ego words. They do not surface from the soul level, the level of love; rather, they surface from the level of fear. Pay attention to your thoughts as you examine the collage. Try to stay *soulful* as you attempt to gain the wisdom reflected from this mirror image of your inner self.

As you reflect on your overall collage, try to get a sense of a theme that may be surfacing. Just as in a dream, a theme often appears in artwork, especially in a collage. What is the message regarding your overall definition of spirituality? Have you used a number of pictures with basically the same images? What might that indicate? As you reflect on your finished product, note any significance in the relationships of one or more of the pictures to any of the other pictures, as well as to the whole collage. Does the collage look empty or overfilled? Does this indicate a life that is too full or not full enough? People who feel overwhelmed and overburdened often design very full collages. When this is the case, it can be valuable to identify what you can now let go of to enable the radiance of your "background" color to show through. If your collage looks too empty, you might ponder what important pieces need to be added to enhance your life. Recall that this collage was to determine your personal definition of spirituality. A question to ponder in that regard might be "What would make my life more spiritually fulfilling?"

Are any pictures placed over top of each other, covering up, blocking some parts from being seen? What might this indicate? Are any pictures not touching anything else on the collage? Sometimes pictures that appear "apart from" depict areas of life that feel separate from other areas of our life. Is there a need to connect these aspects to the total picture of who you are as a spiritual being?

If there are words on the collage, try to make as many sentences as you can with them. Powerful messages are often hidden within the words that appear. Taking the time to view them differently, to "see" them as soul might see them rather than as the cognitive left brain perceives them, can be quite revealing.

Did you place anything on the back of your collage? An item on the back is often a strong reflection of what is pushing or driving us forward at this time. Journal as completely as possible any new awareness you have acquired.

Any art form can be a powerful tool for bringing messages from the subconscious to conscious awareness. Because a collage is so easy and unthreatening to make, I employ the technique frequently in my work with others. I have them build collages around many themes whenever there is a need to receive inner guidance and wisdom. I also create many collages of my own. I have learned that collages, like dreams, can speak to us of where we have been, thus reminding us of what has helped to fashion the circumstances we are now facing. The story that appears can draw our attention to what it is we are now working on at a soul level and can project to us our future. I assembled my first collage about 10 years ago, and I have become what was then being reflected to me.

Many of our dreams appear in three distinct scenes or parts. When we examine these parts, we are often able to identify how the segments indicate our past, our present, and our future. This is true of collage as well. Examine your collage as though it is the road through your spiritual life. Look at the pictures on the left. Do they describe a definition that seems closely related to the beliefs you received from others—your spiritual past, as it were? Were they perhaps influenced by your religious upbringing? Next examine the pictures in the center. Do they seem to more closely represent your current view of spirituality? The immediate centre of a collage generally represents that which is of primary importance at this particular time in life. It is often what we spend a great deal of time focusing on, or it is perhaps what soul is trying to get us to focus on. Examine the pictures on the right. Do these pictures depict aspects of spirituality of which you are still a little unsure— your future definition, so to speak? The theme of most three-part dreams is to show us the past circumstances that have brought us to this particular point in time and to demonstrate what will manifest if the energy we are putting forth continues in like manner. Collage is similar. Reexamine any collage work you have previously done and try to identify a three-part theme. Does the left indicate past experiences, the middle your present, and the right possibilities for your future?

Please note that the ways in which I have invited you to divide and view your collage is rooted in Western Culture wherein the major movement progression is left to right (as in reading). This may not apply if you belong to a culture wherein the dominant progression is right to left or up to down. Sequential time progression—past, present, future—might then need consideration within the context of your culture.

Now divide the collage into three equal sections from bottom to top. The upper section of a collage frequently reflects goals, dreams, and aspirations—ideas that are still not well formed in our mind. They frequently appear in collages as cloudy, foggy, misty, or veiled. The foreground often depicts our foundation, paradigm or supports. Do the pictures in the foreground represent the building blocks upon which your life is built?

Identify pictures that are tilted or placed sideways or perhaps even upside down. Are the aspects they represent somewhat off kilter at this time? Pictures on a collage that are placed in a position different from the way that we normally view them can indicate that something about what they represent is altered, tilted, shifted, or shifting. This can mean that a shift is taking place in the way we see that reality, in the way we are beginning to think about that reality, or in our actions toward that reality. This can also mean that perhaps a shift is necessary at this time to get things more on an even keel, to get things in better balance.

What insights does this information provide? Journal any newly acquired awareness.

You might also like to invite a trusted friend to ask questions of your placement of pictures and then offer feedback as he or she listens to your responses. Take to heart only those comments that instantly feel true, and allow yourself to disregard any that do not. Remember that this is your "soul's work," and although companions can sometimes more readily see what we are blinded from, be sure that when you ask for their impressions, they stay focused on the intent of your collage, which is to identify your particular definition of spirituality. If ego language is offered, a gentle reminder to your partner to stay "soul focused" will be to the advantage of both of you.

Generally speaking, when we offer guidance, it is almost always more empowering and more effective to ask questions rather than to directly state our opinions. Therefore, as you invite another to focus on your collage, encourage him or her to ask questions regarding your soul's reflection. If you are the companion, as you focus on his or her soul's work, remember to pose your statements in a tentative rather than an absolute manner. If there is much spiritual growth and change taking place for either or both of you, there will also likely be shifting and therefore some confusion about your personal definitions of soul, spirit, religion, and spirituality.

How we define these words and the other phrases we use to describe spirituality has much to do with our culture, our faith orientation, and our individual spiritual growth and awareness. For some, spirituality includes a religious orientation; for others, spirituality refers to a personal relationship with a Higher Being. Others define spirituality as that part of the self where the search for meaning takes place. For some, spirituality is an identification of the creative force within the self. Others see the spiritual dimension as relating to one's inner resources and ultimate concerns. Some view this dimension as relating to the basic value around which all other values are focused—the central philosophy of life that guides a person's conduct. Others include the supernatural and nonmaterial dimension of human nature in their definition, whereas many others believe that a person's need to find answers to questions about the meaning of life, illness, and death is an essential aspect of spirituality.[1,2,3,4,5] Reexamine your collage and attempt to identify whether and how your definition includes any or all of the components listed in these generalized group definitions.

Until the end of the 1980s scholars made little distinction between the concepts of spirituality and religion, but by the early 1990s academics were struggling to express a growing awareness of the difference between these concepts.[6] A literature review conducted in 1992 revealed that most authors had defined religion in terms of practices, in terms of dogmas and creeds, and in terms of rites and rituals.[7]

The word *religion* comes from the root phrase meaning "to bind together,"[8] and studies have demonstrated a direct relationship between religion and social support[9] as well as between faith and health.[10, 11] It is unclear, though, how *faith* was defined in the studies. Did those interviewed define faith in terms of their personal spiritual journey, or did they identify faith in terms of remaining *faithful* to a particular religious creed and dogma?

In essence, by being human, all people are spiritual, regardless of whether or how they participate in religious observation.[12] People can be very religious and have very low levels of spirituality; they can be very spiritual and have very low levels of religious practice; they can have low levels of spirituality as well as low levels of religious activity. Others may have high levels of spirituality as well as be highly active in religious practice.[13]

Since ages past, authors and poets, and, more recently, academics, have emphasized that inherent in the human experience is a gnawing desire for a connection with the Divine and a connection to that which is sacred. Most indicate that although all people have a spiritual dimension to their life, there is considerable uniqueness in how they express this aspect of life.

In light of the above, it is necessary to question the ways in which health care professionals assess for spiritual concerns or the need for spiritual care. Does, for example, checking or leaving blank a person's religious affiliation on a history form provide meaningful information about a person's spirituality or assess for indications of spiritual distress?[14] This is a necessary question to ponder deeply as we move into a paradigm that honors more completely the spiritual aspects of human beings.

Has your own definition of spirituality changed recently? Has any particular event been the catalyst for the spiritual shift that is taking or has taken place? Think of others you know who are questioning the status quo of their belief systems and exploring alternate forms of spirituality. What propelled their forward movement?

People who receive professional care services are often in the midst of crisis. It is well recognized that crisis can propel us on an inward journey.[15, 16, 17, 18] The time within is a testing time in which we challenge beliefs and weigh them against our lived experiences, and they often do not hold up under scrutiny. The intensity of the inner anguish is well recognized[19, 20, 21] and is often referred to as *the soul's dark night*, a term coined by John of the Cross.[22] The spiritual crisis is a time of intense spiritual distress, yet the literature reveals that many must walk this difficult path unaccompanied.[23, 24]

During my doctoral studies I read numerous articles on the spiritual void that has over the past decades been so prevalent in the design and delivery of human caring. The authors called for professionals to pay more attention to the spiritual concerns of those within their care; yet, although many of the articles included a definition of spirituality that offered food for thought, none seemed to resonate with the knowing that was unfolding within me. Although they began to acknowledge the need for the spiritual in people's lives, most of the authors continued in their attempts to place spirituality within the framework of organized religion.

Most authors still were unable to step beyond the framework created by the belief system into which they had been indoctrinated. In supporting those seeking spiritual interventions, they continued to offer only interventions that flowed from religious models. As human beings, we long to advance as spiritual beings. Religion can serve us well by connecting us to a group of believers who support our spiritual growth in particular ways and during particular portions of our spiritual journey. As we advance spiritually, we may, however, need spiritual nourishment that our religion and the fellowship of others who practice that religion are no longer able to fully provide. Many of the authors of the articles on spiritual needs seemed unaware that those who move through difficult life experiences struggle with agonizing questions that pour forth from the cracks that are forming in the armor of their beliefs. They appeared not to recognize that it is the belief's crisis that triggers the soul's pain. They appeared not to comprehend that it is not during our "sunny days," but rather during our "dark nights" that we turn inward in an attempt to discover the true meaning and purpose of our lives. The research literature generally was lacking in the presentation of an awareness that the crisis is a manifestation of soul stretching, that the crisis creates the energy needed to shift the personal perspective, and that the crisis is often the catalyst for incredible soul growth.

To be able to work from within a more spiritual paradigm and help others find inner freedom, it is necessary to examine and expand definitions of spirituality that have not changed since childhood. To assist at a soul level, it is essential to define spirituality beyond the boundaries and limits of religious models, regardless of the religion.

Reexamine your collage. Do any pictures hang over the edge? This is usually a sign of growth, a sign of expansion, a sign of stretching. It can indicate that our views no longer fit the "container" in which they are held. Has your particular framework become too small? Recall your intention in creating this collage: It was to determine your particular definition of spirituality. What container has become too small? From what do you need to step forth? This is a positive sign of spiritual growth. During workshops I sometimes see people struggle with the placement of a picture that seems to want to be placed over the edge, but to make it "fit properly," the person will trim the edges. If this happened to you, it would be valuable to ponder what you tried to squeeze in. What in your life no longer fits into your definition of spirituality? What are you trying to squeeze into a model that soul is trying to get you to expand? Spirituality is often depicted as an ever-expanding spiral. In contrast, religions have borders; religious beliefs are limited to particular dogmas and creeds and practices. Is it time to expand outside these parameters?

For a number of years I offered programs for women who were grieving deeply. All of them had experienced significant and, in many cases, lifelong trauma. I heard in their life narratives elements of my own story; I heard their soul pain. In many ways it mirrored my own. Because of my own trauma, because of my own soul pain, and because of the soul healing work that I had been doing personally as well as with others. I recognized I had something of value to offer. I knew I could address their soul pain. I knew I could help them to heal at the deepest of levels. Because left brain psychoeducational approaches had been of little value to me in that regard, I suspected that such approaches would also be of little, if any, value in helping the women to address and heal their souls' pain. Although I knew that left brain hemisphere strategies supply cognitive information, and that the women needed knowledge to help them to understand the various aspects of trauma and recovery, I also knew that, to touch their souls, I needed to incorporate soulful techniques. I was familiar with the research that correlates right brain hemisphere techniques with healing and knew, at a personal level, what the right brain creative endeavors, including the arts, music, dancing, drumming, visualization, and guided imagery, had provided to me.

I dared. I introduced them to the arts and other right brain healing strategies. They became my teachers, my guides. They taught me much about trauma, abuse, grief, sorrow, regret, and shame. They taught me much about love and beauty and soul. The right brain strategies gave voice to their souls,[25] and in turn they gave voice to the ever-increasing awareness growing within me.

At the start of every new program, I invited each woman to identify what spirituality meant to her personally. Before doing an artful activity to further explore this concept, and as a way to have each woman recognize her own knowing and honor her own strengths in this area, I gave each a blank sheet of gold-colored paper. I asked the women to list all of the words that are necessary to include in a personal definition of spirituality and then to create a collage to depict their definition. When they had completed the activities, I invited the women to share their words and the pictures that represented them, while a cofacilitator transcribed the words that reflected their "inner knowing" onto a flipchart.

After completing seven programs of *Journey to Hope and Healing: Beyond Trauma and Abuse*,[26] I engaged an assistant to examine the lists and identify any themes that might have surfaced. Definite themes emerged—themes that indicated that the women in these groups saw spirituality as different from religion. They viewed spirituality as a personal and individual journey that they described as a discovering of the Divine within themselves, within others, and within all of creation.

You might like to reexamine the collage you just created. Does your collage include pictures to indicate a difference between spirituality and religion, or do you see these concepts as being one and the same? Does your collage include pictures that depict a belief that you are an important aspect of your definition of spirituality? Do the pictures on your collage reveal an acknowledgement that other human beings are also important in a definition of spirituality? Does your definition of spirituality, expressed through your collage, reflect aspects of nature, the elements, and the animal and bird kingdoms? Does your collage in some way depict a connection between you and the Creator?

How do you visualize this connection? Return to your art supplies and complete a further **art activity**. To do so you will need a number of colored markers and a poster-paper-size piece of paper. You might also like to gather some decorative materials, including glitter dust, ribbon and stickers for this activity.

Before you begin, sit for about 10 minutes in silence, listening to some meditative music. Allow the music to fill you. Allow yourself to become one with the music. As you do so, ponder: "How am I connected to the Divine?" "What does my connection with the Divine look like?" Allow the answers to flow through you. Do not try to control the outcome. When you feel ready, draw, design, or decorate whatever images come to mind. Continue the process until you feel complete. The feeling of total completion may come before the feeling of total satisfaction. If you feel this incongruence, just allow it to be so.

When you feel complete, take a break. Perhaps go for a walk in nature, and after an hour or so return to your creation. Record in your journal the answers that surface as you reflect on what your creation reveals. What feelings did you have the first moment that you looked at the picture? What thoughts followed these initial sensations?

What does your creation look like? What does it reflect to you? What colors appear? How did you image the Creator or Creative Force? Are aspects of the cosmos or a greater universe present? Did any symbols appear? Did you design circles, squares, triangles, hexagons, octagons, swirls? Did you draw a sun, stars, moons, or other images of light? Did you draw a rainbow? Did any of the elements surface—fire, wind, water, rocks; the heavens, Earth? Did you draw trees or other plant life, insects such as butterflies or dragonflies, birds, or animals? Does your creation contain images of buildings or sacred sites?

Does the image that poured from you and which is now portrayed before you whisper of an innate knowledge of a connection between Creator, you, others, and all aspects of creation?

Reflect on what is revealed and then journal your impressions.

Turn your picture and examine it from top to bottom and from side to side. Identify any new images that appear. Hang your picture on a wall and step back. From several distances, identify and journal any new images, thoughts, or sensations that come. Reflect on what is revealed. Journal any further impressions that present themselves.

Were you able to externalize in art form a connection with the Creator and the Creative Force? If you were to use this picture to define this connection, what would you write? As you gaze at your creation, do you experience an increased sense of Oneness with the Divine?

Consider your life and life circumstance. As you do, ask yourself, "Where is God in all of this?"

Did you have an Aha! experience? Note in your journal any new insights that you gained. Write in detail any plaguing questions that surface. You will want to return to these questions in the future. Each time you do so, ask the same question of yourself and record your new answers. Then return to this first set of answers and compare the two sets. In that way you will be able to use this exercise as a measure of spiritual progress.

Did you initially experience a powerful and positive image and/or sensation that you immediately rejected? In other words, did your right brain—your soul brain—resonate instantly with the symbolic messages in your drawing? And, upon receiving this right brain knowing, did your left brain immediately challenge it?

As I stated previously and will reemphasize in future chapters, soul recognizes truth. Soul knows truth in an instant. Soul messages encourage us to look at the truth, to examine who we really are. Soul is always encouraging us to reevaluate the direction of our lives. Soul is always trying to move us forward in a positive way.

Learning to recognize and then to trust our first thoughts is powerful. When we have been wounded, we lose trust in ourselves and in our own abilities. Reawakening to the voice of soul helps immensely in alleviating the anxiety that comes with feeling broken and disconnected. A soul thought always encourages, always tells of the awesomeness that we are. Soul thoughts communicate: "Wow! You can do it! Go for it! You're worth it! Do it!" Soul thoughts are based in love, in abundance, and in goodness. Soul messages reinforce Oneness.

Return to your drawing and label it *My Divine Connection*. Reexamine your initial response, your gut instincts, your first thought as you saw your own drawing. Trust this response. Trust that what is revealed is of great significance. The power in knowing and experiencing Oneness is to know and experience love and belonging. When we truly know, understand, and experience our Divine Connection, fear no longer controls us. Love is always about belonging. Fear is always about separation. The more we feel separate and apart from the Divine and from the Divine Energy in All, the less we trust the universal order. The less we trust the universal order, the less we are able to take risks. The less able we are to risk, the less able we are to move our lives in the direction of healing, in the direction of our spiritual purpose.

Return to your art table for a further **art activity**. This time select a sheet of gold paper. Draw a circle to fit the page. Now close your eyes and imagine that this gold circle is your soul in all its brightness and in full awareness of its connection to the Divine, of its own Divinity. Now, for a few moments recall all of your life's hurts. Think of all the difficult life experiences you have had, all of the losses. Recall not only the losses of loved ones, but also losses of dreams and goals, opportunities, and promotions. Think also of losses of self-worth and courage, trust, hope, and love. Ponder losses of childhood, sexuality, spirituality, community, culture. Focus on any loss of body parts or functions. Whatever your losses, whatever it is you grieve, think of how that would look if you were to place it on this circle. Reflect on how much energy it takes to deal with each particular loss. Decide, and then slice the circle in pie-like sections, each piece sized according to the loss it represents. Create each section in the color and shape that best depicts the loss it represents.

When you feel complete, spend some time pondering this experience and what it means to you and then journal the experience and any new awareness that you have gained.

Now reexamine each wedge section and reflect on the degree of healing already done around each of the losses represented there. Take some stickers that would best represent the healing work you have already done around each of the losses, and place the appropriate sticker or stickers on that section. When you have completed this portion of the activity, journal as completely as possible the meaningfulness of this activity; be sure to reflect on what it felt like to honor your losses as well as to acknowledge the healing work that you have done.

There is great value in naming our losses and taking the time to honor our woundedness. I believe that one of the reasons that we have a difficult time moving forward in life is that we have never given ourselves permission to acknowledge our pain and recognize the soul effects of difficult life experiences. I also believe that few people recognize the healing they have already done. I frequently ask wounded people to complete their Circle of Significance[27] to honor their life's challenges and acknowledge the forward movement they have made. It is empowering to recognize the strengths gained as we reflect upon our individual journeys through pain and healing.

As you ponder your own Circle of Significance reflect on the relationship between any healing that you have done and your spiritual journey. Do you see a relationship? Do you recognize how hurt and pain cover your golden essence? Have you gained a heightened desire for personal healing and to assist others in uncovering their golden essence?

To emphasize this point further, you might like to take a few more moments to complete a further **art activity**. This time use paints or markers to depict what brokenness might look like. As soon as you have completed your drawing of brokenness, immediately draw another image on top of "brokenness" that would change brokenness to wholeness. Then take a new sheet of paper and quickly draw a picture depicting what healing would look like should you be able to capture it with colors. As soon as you have completed the drawing of healing, change the picture so that it depicts soul growth. Now examine the two completed pictures. What are the similarities and what are the differences between the final products? Did your choice of colors change? Did your choice of colors change to brighter colors or to lighter colors as you depicted soul growth? While there is significance to the colors you used, there are no right or wrong color choices. The meanings of colors are interpreted in various ways depending on the color systems applied by the interpreter. As you read further, you will likely gain more understanding of your particular color choices.

Do you see in your artwork relationships amongst the concepts of brokenness, healing spirituality, and wholeness? Return to all of the artwork that you have completed since the beginning of this chapter. Is there evidence that your soul is encouraging you to recognize these connections?

I now acknowledge no difference between the concepts. For me, the healing journey and the spiritual journey are one and the same.[28] My healing journey was an intense search for spiritual truth. In *Journey to the Sacred: Mending a Fractured Soul*[29] I tell of my struggles with untested beliefs following the tragic death of my son. I relate my search to find a definition for spirituality that fits the knowing surfacing within me. In that book I described how, while gazing at the Golden Buddha and listening to the profound history unearthed around the artifact, I found a metaphor to describe my spiritual journey. From that I created a personal definition appropriate to the awakening to spiritual truths that was taking place in my life.

In 1954 the Golden Buddha that now stands in Traimitwitthayaram Temple in Bangkok was chipped from beneath a clay disguise. As I listened to the guide relate this incredible story, I knew that I was being offered a mirrored reflection of my own life. Although at that time I was only beginning to recognize such messages, I knew that this message was of great significance. I knew that I was being guided to pay full attention.

My search for ways to heal the deep pain lodged within my soul led me to seek ways to unearth the sacred in my own life, but it was not until I pondered the Golden Buddha story that I recognized that, like the Golden Buddha, my real self, my golden self was hidden beneath mounds of clay. My clay was created out of fear and hurt, guilt and regret. I knew that I could not access or truly get in touch with the real me until I had chipped away the clay disguise. As I gazed upon the sacred relic, I acknowledged that my spiritual journey was a journey to discover my golden essence. And also, like the clay Buddha, the more I chipped away the clay that was encasing me, protecting me, I believed, from the world, from further hurt, the more my gold was revealed. As cracks formed in the chink, I recognized that more of my Light was radiating outward, becoming increasingly visible to those around me. The more I freed myself from my clay wrappings, the more I knew of my true nature, and the more I was able to draw in more and more Divine Light. I was then better able to capture glimpses of that same Light being radiated to me from the Divineness in other beings and all other forms in creation—the rocks, trees, clouds, and stars.

My healing journey evolved, without my conscious awareness, into a spiritual journey. The journey that led me within, although long and arduous, ultimately became a journey of remembering who I was. My journey within was a journey of rediscovering and of reclaiming my Golden Essence, my True Essence, my Divine Essence. It was remembering that the Spirit, the Life Energy that created all things, also created me; and even now it continues to flow through me. It is a part of me. I came to know that my Spirit, my Life Energy is a part of the Creative Energy, the Creative Force. I had come to know that the Fire of Creation burns deep within me, that my Spirit, my Life Energy, is a part of the same Life Energy that penetrates all living things, even the burning core deep within the Earth. I am a part of the Life Force of the Creator and of all that has been created.

Has your life experience resulted in a similar understanding? Reexamine the artwork that you have completed since you began this chapter. Is this inner knowing revealed?

The symbol of the Golden Buddha reminded me that, like the clay used to protect its True Essence within, heavy castings of hurt and pain obstruct our radiance from shining forth, hindering others from seeing our Creative Fire. It likewise blocks the light being reflected to us from those around us. Happily, it takes only a few chinks before a gleam can be picked up from the torch of another.

Because of this awareness, I began to recognize that spirituality is also a journey of relating. The journey deep within the cavern of clay, to discover there our Eternal Flame, becomes a catalyst for the journey without. Once our flame is fanned, the energy from the ever-increasing brilliance penetrates and begins to erode our clay envelope. We become a beacon. Others readily pick up our light, and we begin to detect their gleam being sent our way. The ever-increasing vibrations from our ever-increasing internal fire draws, not only those who resonate in synchrony, but also those who see within us a light that can rekindle their own.

The more I acknowledged and connected with the Light within myself and others, the more I recognized that spirituality is also a journey of reconnecting, for I was being drawn not only to the light in other people, but also to the splendor that surrounded me. As I realized that everything in creation contains the Divine Light, I began to resonate more and more with the wonder and expanse of the universe and to increasingly pay attention to the "awfulness" of the Sacred Fire in all of creation.

The affirmation and numerous other unnamable treasures I received from the participants in the groups with whom I worked and from those with whom I "walked" during individual therapeutic sessions gave me the courage to give voice to my personal discovery of the spiritual truths that I unearthed and to share this learning for the soul healing of others. In affirming their efforts, I affirmed my own. I now confidently define spirituality as a triune journey to rediscover the three Rs of life: Remembering, Relating, and Reconnecting.

This is the definition of spirituality I now live by; it is the definition upon which I base the soul work that I do. I trust that you too will find it a worthy definition upon which to base the soul-healing work that you already do and that you are about to undertake in a more in-depth and conscious way.

# CHAPTER 5

# CHALLENGING EXISTING MODELS OF HELPING

*Many men build as cathedrals are built,*
*the part nearest the ground finished,*
*But the parts that soar toward the heavens—*
*the turrets and the spires—forever incomplete.*

H. W. Beecher

Returning to Canada following my study in Hawaii was difficult in numerous ways. It was confusing to be a foreigner in the land of my birth. I felt some culture shock following my relocation to the islands, but the confusion and disorientation that I felt upon returning to my homeland was immense. Of the greatest significance, however, was how acutely aware I was of the many and numerous circumstances in which I felt displaced—out of touch with everything that had once been familiar. My experiences and study of spirituality had changed me. The immersion in the Hawaiian culture, including the slower pace of life, the focus on values, and the Islanders' immense understanding of the spiritual, of healing and wholeness, and of family and family life were quite different from those honored and revered in much of mainland North America.

Although adjusting to every aspect of living seemed difficult, nowhere was this more profound than in my work setting. My education and experience had prepared me more than adequately for the position accepted, but it took little time to recognize the poor fit, the chaos and disharmony between my internal and external worlds. It was as though I had been dropped into a setting in another time and place. I felt alien, separate, and apart.

My longing for some of the spiritual warmth I experienced in Hawaii led me to the Hispanic community. Recognizing the value in learning to read, write, and speak their language, I enrolled in a Spanish class. The teacher was a refugee who told numerous stories of the atrocities he had experienced in his country. He expressed his gratefulness for being able to live in a place where he and his family were safe and where his sons could receive education and therefore the promise of successful futures. He also, however, shared numerous stories of intense soul pain—feelings of being disconnected from all that was important to him. He had been a university professor, but because his teaching credentials were not recognized in Canada, he was unable to acquire a position in his much-loved profession. In an effort to support his family, he held three part-time jobs. Those with whom he worked had little comprehension of his background, his joys and his sorrows, his successes and his failures. They knew little of the country and the life style he knew and longed for. They knew even less of the world where he now dwelt in grief. They knew nothing at all of the man and his soul's longing.

Perhaps no other person in the class heard his stories the way that I heard them. Perhaps no one else remembers him today or could recall any of his stories. I know them all by heart. His narratives resonated deeply within my own soul, and they touch me yet today. His soul pain mirrored my own, and like the older persons whose stories I related in a previous chapter, his longing to feel a sense of belonging, his longing to know and be known were immense. No one knew who he really was. No one knew what he desired to offer the world. No one knew his life experiences or what his education had prepared him for. He, like I, felt abandoned and alone, adrift on the great sea of life.

Our workplaces and institutions are filled with human beings who require us to make a difference. To make a difference, to hear their soul pain, to help them be soulfully free, we must be willing to shift our focus. We must see beyond the biophysical, even beyond their psychosocial concerns. We must view human beings in different ways. To truly make a difference, we must see the wholeness, not just give lip service to the notion of wholeness, but we must truly see and respond to the body, mind, and soul concerns of each human we encounter, ourselves included. Only when we are able to do so can we shift our perspective to the place where we can address the deepest concerns, the soul concerns.

Yet, we often continue to work strictly from within the models with which we are familiar. This provides not only safety (because even the thought of change can cause us to feel anxiety and a loss of control), but also a thick blanket of insulation that keeps us from facing, and therefore addressing, those socially important problems that are not reducible to the puzzle forms that our models prescribe. For example, if the soul concerns that institutionalized older persons express cannot be stated in terms of the jargon we have been trained to use, or measured by the instruments that the models designed for our practice supply, we can disregard their concerns and label them as *unfit*; for indeed, they do not fit our view. We can therefore insulate ourselves from their problems. And when we do that, it becomes unnecessary to find solutions. For why would we seek solutions to problems when the models designed to guide the actions of those who subscribe to them blind the observer from seeing those problems?

Most of us do not like to acknowledge that we insulate ourselves from the problems of others; yet the major way of reinforcing our view of the world, and the models and methods used to sustain that perspective, serves to increase the insulation. When things are going smoothly and most people around us hold similar beliefs and have similar experiences, there is no need to examine our beliefs and our actions. Only when our worldview is challenged are we in a position to identify how microscopic or how expansive our vision really is. Only when our beliefs are threatened do we increase the insulation—the walls, the protecting factors around us. When our beliefs are threatened,—when, for example, we recognize that things are not as they seem and know that change is required,—we increase our blindness, for our blindness provides the best insulation. And when we remain blind to the real problems around us, we can feel justified in not stepping out in courage, in not offering what we can, in not making the necessary changes.

We reinforce our blindness and therefore our insulation through practices of exclusion. The stronger our need to block, the better we become at excluding those who do not "fit." Our numerous excluding behaviors include avoidance techniques, such as ignoring, pretending we do not hear, ensuring that we remain too busy. They also include labeling and judging statements that we communicate verbally, nonverbally, or in written form.

They include advising statements that we make in the hope of "fixing" another to make him or her more acceptable to the norms. They include the acceptance of and acting on diagnoses we know are inaccurate or incomplete, and they include the numerous other ways in which we bar those who need assistance and support from receiving assistance in ways that would be truly meaningful and helpful.

To make a difference, we must be willing to remove the insulation that separates us from others. Insulating ourselves from the pain of others happens not only in our institutions, but also in many of life's settings. Many insulate themselves, for example, from really seeing the correlations between violence and its causes. Many seem unable to relate to the relationships between violence, the drug trade, and prostitution. Many refuse to acknowledge that repeated trauma can lead to the abuse of drugs and alcohol. It is easier to remain blind to the fact that drugs and alcohol are frequently used to numb the emotional, mental, and spiritual pain resulting from child and spousal abuse than to step out from behind our protective walls and step toward changing the structures that support such behaviors. It is simpler to side with the power than to side with those who are powerless. So, although ever-increasing numbers of researchers and clinicians[1] have described the relationships between abuse and violence and the use of drugs, and the need to prostitute to pay for the habit, the laws in most nations continue to ignore this vicious cycle and spend few resources on preventing abuse or on healing the tremendous wounds that result from crimes of violence. Is it less complicated to reinforce insulation than to help to alter the United Nations' statistics? Its reports indicate that the global sex trade generates more than $12 billion a year.[2] What will it take before we, as a world community, act in ways that change these findings, act in ways that release those in sexual captivity?

Many women in our penitentiaries and mental illness facilities have life histories of abuse and trauma. They frequently relate feelings and experiences that indicate soul trauma. Yet the solutions most commonly prescribed flow from treatment regimes created from within models that do not recognize soul concerns. Strictly applying the strategies and techniques of such models clearly demonstrates in one more way the power of our worldview to see, or to blind us from seeing, the reality around us. Because many of the currently used practice models focus attention almost exclusively on viewing maladaptive behaviors as biopsychosocial illnesses, we view other concerns or symptoms that do not quite fit this framework as metaphysical or too intangible to be worth the while. How different might it be should we begin to address manifestations of spiritual distress with techniques developed from within a spiritual framework?

The years following the death of my son were incredibly difficult. I desperately tried in the beginning to hang on to old beliefs and old ways of functioning. As time went on, this became increasingly more difficult. An awareness of what I really needed for healing was growing within me. What I was searching for and longing for had much more to do with the soul pain that was oozing forth from the deep and rugged fissures of my fractured soul than it had to do with the emotional or physical manifestations of grief. Yet every grief book I read and every grief group or workshop I attended addressed only these concerns. Even my associates and the professionals from whom I sought assistance could offer no more. All shared their understanding of grief. All focused on concerns that were no longer my concerns. My soul was starving. No one seemed able to offer the food I needed to feed my ravenous spirit.

Those of us educated over the past several decades in the Western world were indoctrinated into a worldview that grew out of the scientific approach. This approach taught the necessity of focusing on objective data, on the tangible and quantifiable. This equated with emphasizing the observable, and therefore, the most easily measured. Health care and allied health care professionals were introduced to theories and models that supported this deduction. The model that Abraham Maslow[3] developed became one of choice for many professionals, for it guided the framework development for their education and for the service delivery in the health-related organizations in which they had interned. This model directs that human beings have needs that are hierarchical in nature, meaning that we must attain lower-order needs prior to achieving higher-end needs. Maslow's hierarchical needs model was designed in pyramidal form. The largest portion of the pyramid houses the lower-end needs, with the small tip portion accommodating the highest-end needs. The *needs* that Maslow identified are laddered on the pyramid in the order in which they must be attained. Progression of movement is from the biological, to safety and security, to love and belonging, to esteem, and then to self-actualization. According to this philosophy, only after human beings have attained the lower-end needs do they aspire for the goal of self-actualization—spiritual fulfillment.

As I began walking beside people in emotional crises, I had great difficulty applying Maslow's model to their experiences. Although many of those who sought help with their grief and their trauma survived on less than sufficient resources for food and housing, and many struggled in the turmoil of their relationships, these were not their paramount concerns. They spent most of their energy trying to figure out the "God" questions in their lives. They pondered about and sought help for the "why" questions that continually nagged them for answers. My most profound awareness as I began to work with people who had been significantly wounded was how spiritually insightful they were. I learned to pay attention and to gain from the knowledge they shared. Many had worked though the hard ground of some very difficult emotional and spiritual hills. They had challenged many of their old beliefs and were presenting with a knowing that was now truly theirs. I heard in their musings and ponderings the soul queries I myself wrestled with. I identified with the truths they shared. These were people in crisis. If I had applied a needs model, many would have been categorized as having numerous physical needs, yet their energy was being invested in the needs of the highest order. These people were, according to Maslow's hierarchy, working on self-actualization. Many of them shared peak experiences as they related newly found insights.

Yet, guided by Maslow's model and others that similarly emphasize that physical needs must be met prior to the attainment of the higher-order needs, professionals and professional organizations have for decades focused great amounts of energy in terms of human and financial resources on attempting to meet the physical needs of the populace. Even though there has been considerable sociological evidence of the futility of these efforts and the learned helplessness that results from this focus, the majority of professionals and professional organizations remain tied to their commitments to these models.

Following the completion of my doctoral studies, I was offered a position in which I was to teach the promotion of health. I was grateful for the opportunity, for as a clinician, I witnessed numerous examples of how practices that developed within these models interfered with people's innate abilities and drive for wholeness. I also noted that the influences that pervaded the Western approach to humankind and human care also invaded humankind's own view of itself. In many ways we all lost sight of our wholeness. Many did not acknowledge that as human beings we manifest our spirituality in body, mind, and emotions and that we coexist with every aspect of our social and natural environments.

In an effort to teach health-promotion philosophy as completely as possible, I formulated a working definition that I based upon my own experiences in using holistic methods of healing. I defined well-being as "positive striving toward balance within and between the physical, emotional, intellectual, and spiritual aspects of our humanness and the social and natural environments."[4] The literature emphasized that to provide an overall sense of wellness, efforts must focus on attaining well-being in each of the aspects represented in the wellness models. When I reviewed manuals designed to guide health-promotion efforts, I was dismayed, however, to discover that although the wellness approach developed in response to a call for a more holistic approach to life and health, the emphasis continued to be on addressing the physical determinants. The bulk of health-promotion dollars were spent on literature and programs that addressed physical concerns related to the reduction of smoking and to nutrition and exercise. Although the emotional and environmental factors that interfere with health and wellness received some recognition, for the most part, the other human aspects, including the intellectual and spiritual aspects of wholeness and the impact of the social environment on the maintenance or disruption of health and wellness, were ignored.

The paradigm was shifting, but those who prescribed the "new worldview" were not able to see the new reality. Their vision was blocked by the walls of a framework that still contained their definition of humanity. The approach they recommended lacked an understanding of healing and holism.

Because in my own journey to healing I had embarked on a course of discovering the spiritual aspects of life and wholeness, and because I had just completed a doctoral dissertation in which I explored, in depth, the concepts of spirituality and spiritual well-being, I found the huge gap in the wellness information disconcerting. In an effort to address this dilemma and fill this void, at least in the material I presented, I spent long hours reviewing the wellness models and pondering the association of these concepts with my notions of spiritual well-being.

I knew spiritual distress well. I knew it personally. For years it had been my ever-constant companion. I knew of unfulfilled spiritual needs, for they had constituted my life. I knew insecurity and feelings of being unsafe when

I was no longer able to trust a God, trust myself, trust others, or trust the universal order. I knew of the struggle with self-worth and with feelings of being unworthy of love. I knew hopelessness. I knew helplessness. I knew the need to feel forgiven and the need for self-forgiveness. I spent years on a first-name basis with guilt, shame, and regret. I knew anger. I knew the fear of having anger for the God who allowed such pain. I knew the struggle to find ways to release such intense fear and anger. I knew the separation that this created in my life. I knew abandonment. I knew feelings of being disconnected, of being separate and apart. I knew what it was to lose my sense of identity, and I knew the agony of the search in the darkest of places, looking for what I was to be and to become. I knew the effort required to find unused talents and abilities. I knew the possibility of failure.

I knew brokenness of spirit!

More significantly, I also knew the journey to wholeness.

I walked hundreds of miles seeking my soul's energy. While I searched, I connected with the universe. I found the Creator in the stars and in the meadows, and there I found love and hope and joy and forgiveness. I found peace in my garden, and I developed a desire for the energy-filled foods my garden produced. I found health for my physical body. I found meditation. And deep within the recesses of my inner self, I discovered unused talents and creative abilities and the courage to risk.

As I reflected upon my own journey, I became aware of how during my times of spiritual distress every aspect of my humanness had been affected, and I realized that as my journey to soul healing advanced, wellness in each of the other aspects advanced as well.

To present a model of wellness that did not address these notions and feelings was, for me, a model that did not recognize what it is that interferes with people's journey to wellness and ultimate wholeness. To present a model that asked people only to monitor their nutrition to lose weight was dishonoring of my own journey to wholeness and of the journey of those I was walking beside. To teach people to manage their stress with deep breathing and short breaks was blowing smoke off the tip of a volcanic mountain ready to explode.

One day, in a concluding review to a series of presentations that focused on the six aspects of well-being, I plotted each of the well-being aspects in linear form on a whiteboard. I asked the participants (who in this particular group ranged in age from 55 to 88 years) to describe ways in which we can advance wellness in each of these areas. Because we spent a full session on each of the aspects of well-being, the group had little difficulty completing the activity. Under physical wellness they noted "Pay attention to exercise and nutrition"; under emotional wellness they listed "Manage your stress, change negative self-talk to positive self-talk, and use daily affirmations." Under intellectual wellness the group cited examples of being involved in personal learning and work environments that stimulate intellectual growth. Under spiritual wellness they listed the six spiritual needs, but changed the word *need* to *longing*.

The literature on spiritual well-being identified the spiritual needs as the need to give love and receive love unconditionally from God, self, and others; the need to feel a sense of trust with God, self, and others; the need to hope; the need to forgive and receive forgiveness from God, self, and others; the need for connectedness to God and others; and the need to find meaning and purpose in life.[5, 6, 7] I shared with the group that because of my own personal experience and my work with others, I now used the word longing rather than the word need. In changing their own language from need to longing, I knew that they too had embraced this philosophy. When we are in spiritual distress, in a personal place of feeling less than whole spiritually, we long for wholeness. We long to give love and receive love unconditionally; we long to feel a sense of trust; we long to feel hopeful once again; we long to forgive and feel forgiveness; we long to belong, to feel connected. We long for all these things with God, self, and others; and we long to find meaning and purpose in our lives. In responding as they did to this review, the participants were acknowledging their own awareness and perhaps their own personal experiences with longing for spiritual wholeness.

Under social wellness the group indicated the importance of continuing to develop supportive and nurturing relationships. They identified taking classes in effective communication as one way to advance social wellness; and safety and pollution reduction, as well as claiming personal responsibility for caring for the environment, as ways to advance environmental wellness.

Because one of the notions of holism is that all of the dimensions of our humanness are interrelated and interdependent, I proceeded to explore with the group how they viewed the interrelationships between the various aspects in the wellness models. At their invitation, I used spiritual well-being as the example, and although I had never done this before in such a tangible way, I had spent long hours pondering the interrelationships. But even after the hours of intellectual pondering I was enlightened as well as encouraged by what we discovered.

After much dialogue and processing and reprocessing of the week's information and much braiding together of the new information with the life experiences of everyone in the group, we concluded that the spiritual longing for self-love could be an aspect of physical well-being. All members agreed that if we really love ourselves, we care about how we look and feel. Nutrition, exercise, and reducing caffeine, alcohol, and other drugs become important goals when we recognize that we are caring for a "temple that houses such a treasure."

Under emotional well-being the group again chose self-love. They dialogued about the relationship between self-love, self-worth, and self-esteem and about how they are reflected in self-talk. They also included trust and hope and agreed that there was a direct relationship between the degree to which a person could trust and hope and the feelings of emotional wellness, and therefore between emotional and spiritual well-being.

The group acknowledged that when we are unable to trust, it is difficult to take the risks so necessary to move in the direction of intellectual wellness. Under the title of intellectual wellness they placed spiritual longing for meaning and purpose in life. They concluded that to use our talents and abilities to the fullest of our potential, we must be in personal, social, and work environments that support our capabilities. It often takes a great deal of risk and courage to move in and out of relationships in which we are unable to use our gifts and abilities to the fullest. When we are unable to do so, we feel blocked in our growth and long to find ways to express our true selves. We recognize that our purpose in life is being thwarted. The group discovered that the movement to attain social wellness requires the love of others, forgiveness, and a sense of belonging and connectedness, which thus demonstrates a close relationship between social and spiritual well-being.

The study group also dialogued about the soul's longing for connectedness. They discussed how we as a people have been able to reach the moon and return, but find it troublesome to cross the street and meet our neighbors. Some people fill this void by connecting to a community of common faith believers. Their common faith is the glue of connectedness. The need to belong, to feel that one is important and that one matters, is affirmed for many by the traditions and practices of their faith community. The members of the study group described their own strong links with others who held similar beliefs and acknowledged the support that they received from them. They recognized that the need for connection to their faith group seems most significant during times of intense emotion, both during times of great joy and times of intense sorrow—during times of celebration and during times of mourning. The group agreed that the need for belonging and connectedness also extends into their environment. When we celebrate, as well as when we mourn, the community assists in creating the environment we require to fulfill our joy or to help us pour out our sorrow. Music, flowers, and colors are traditional ways through which we use the outward environment to assist the expressions of our internal processes.

The group identified some of the numerous other ways in which as spiritual human beings we are connected to our environment. Many shared personal peak experiences at the ocean, on the rivers, in the mountains, the forests, and the deserts. Some described these moments in nature as the most sacred they experienced. The group suggested that if we really understood our interrelationship to everything in creation, we would each take a greater personal responsibility for creating a safer and more healing environment for ourselves and the generations who will follow.

As a group we acknowledged that when we are spiritually unfulfilled, every aspect of us is affected. When we struggle in soul pain, every aspect of our humanness suffers. Each member of the group grasped the concept of wholeness in a different and more expanded way. We acknowledged that spiritual energy penetrates every aspect of our being and radiates from us, influencing and affecting others and the larger environment. We shared examples of our newfound learning. We discussed how we often experience the need for emotional forgiveness from feelings of guilt and regret. The "heavy blanket of guilt and regret" often manifests in the physical body as pain across the upper back. We succumb to the weight of these difficult emotions, and the signs are revealed in the symptoms of our physical body. The digestive system may begin to have difficulty "swallowing" the unresolved feelings. Sleep disturbances may result from the emotional wrestling, and a lack of sleep soon interferes with mental and intellectual capabilities. When stress and unhappiness are projected, social relationships are affected, and rather than seeking forgiveness, we often choose to escape into cigarettes, caffeine, drugs, and alcohol or act out in aggressive and violent ways. All lead to either damaging our world or placing ourselves and others in unhealthy and often unsafe surroundings.

I designed the group activity for that day to facilitate a more complete understanding of the interconnectedness and interrelatedness of each of the human aspects. My intention was to ensure that the group captured the notion that although human beings are made up of parts, we are much more than the sum of the parts. We are never truly whole when any of the parts are broken, for brokenness affects the whole. Bringing a more complete model of wellness to the participants resulted in an immense knowing. In a very cognitive, tangible, and concrete way we more truly understood holism and our nature as human beings. During this activity we, as a group, articulated in a clear and profound way our understanding of the overlay of our spiritual nature and of how soul joys and soul concerns are reflected in every aspect of our humanness. In recognizing the pervasive influence of our spiritual essence on every aspect of our humanness, we acknowledged in a very significant way the spiritual essence of our human nature. We discovered that brokenness of spirit affects every aspect of our being and that wholeness of the human being is wholeness of soul.

This learning greatly impacted my abilities to see and to respond from a more spiritually based paradigm. The more I looked, the more I saw evidence in my own life of the spiritual thread woven through all my endeavors. The more I taught and counseled others, the more I saw evidence of the desire for spiritual fulfillment as the basis of their quest. Although in most cases people were not using language indicative of being on a spiritual journey, but instead, often used metaphoric and emotional language, as I listened I recognized that hidden beneath the metaphors and emotional expressions was a deep soul yearning. Each time I listened to a wish to advance physical well-being, I found evidence of decreased feelings of guilt, shame, and regret and a corresponding increase in self-acceptance and self-forgiveness. Each time someone expressed a desire to advance intellectually and emotionally, I saw evidence of increased self-love and an increased acceptance of having a Divine purpose. Each time there was a wish to improve relationships or become more connected to nature, I saw an increase in the spiritual aspects of trust and hope and an ability to see the divineness in others and in all creation.

DR. JANE A. SIMINGTON, PH.D

Each time I saw a desire for spiritual fulfillment, I saw forward movement in the ability to give and receive love, to hope, to trust, to forgive, and to receive forgiveness. Each time I saw movement along the spiritual path, I saw an increased sense of belonging and increased feelings of connectedness to others and to all life. And each time I saw an increased sense of belonging, I saw recognition that life did indeed have meaning. And as the meaning was discovered, I saw a search for talents and abilities and a discovery of life's purpose.

In light of this review, I knew that it was time to rearrange the order on the models that guided my practice. It was time to reconstruct the pyramid. It was time to honor the spiritual base of the human beings to whom I was offering service.

## A Different Approach to Helping and Healing

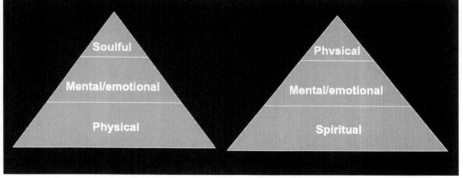

Maslow (1954)                    Simington (2000)

It was time to practice what I knew to be truth. It was time to open windows in both my personal and professional life, to stand on the sill and look far beyond the immediate. It was time to scrutinize through a different lens the data I was gathering. I needed to observe it for alternative causes. I needed to remove my insulation, break down old walls, shift paradigms, and begin in earnest to create a new model, and in so doing discover and promote alternative solutions.

Is it time for you to do the same? It will take great courage, for applying a new model will help to shift a well-entrenched paradigm. Not everyone will be in favor of such a shift, for the application of new models automatically challenges the prevailing worldview and therefore challenges those who have invested much in building and maintaining it.

Like Moses, you will likely ask, "Why will the people listen to me?" and "How can I convince the pharaohs of my day?" And, like Moses, you will risk the possibility of rejection.

If we are to offer our children a more peaceful, safe, and healed world, each of us must somehow find our confidence and trust that, like Moses, when we begin to work within the spiritual dimensions, we too will be given resources that we can only now begin to imagine.[8]

# CHAPTER 6

# VISIONING NEW POSSIBILITIES

*If we are seeing less than half of what is out there,*
*what is out there that we are not seeing?*

Michael Talbot, The Holographic Universe

In *Stalking the Wild Pendulum*, Itzhak Bentov[1] noted:

> We human beings consider ourselves to be made up of 'solid matter.' Actually the physical body is the end product, so to speak, of the subtle information fields, which mold our physical body as well as all physical matter. These fields are holograms which change in time (and are) outside the reach of our normal senses. This is what clairvoyants perceive as colorful egg-shaped halos or auras surrounding our physical bodies.

The following **art activity** and guided imagery will help you grasp these notions more fully. You will require the assistance of a trusted friend to complete it. Be sure to pick someone whose spiritual development is similar to yours. Each of you will need about six feet of paper. Paper used to cover tables at buffet banquets works well. You will also need a variety of colored markers and chalk pastels.

Place the papers on the floor and take turns lying on them. Using a colored marker, trace around each other's physical form.

Spend a few quiet moments reflecting on the phrases "My Divine Light," "My Spiritual Essence." Ponder what these words mean with regard to you specifically. Then take turns reading the guided imagery to each other.

As you begin the imagery, I will invite you to connect with your breath. Numerous cultural, spiritual, and religious teachings surround breath, air, and wind. The Old Testament often referred to, Yahweh, the God of the Jewish people, as the wind. The Great Medicine Wheels of the world generally associate air or wind with the East, the place of new beginnings. Many traditional teachings call attention to the direction from which the winds blow. Winds of the South, for example, invite increased attention to the maintenance of physical strength and endurance. Winds of the West are healing winds; North winds remind us of our ancestors and their wisdom and are an invitation for gratefulness and leadership.

*As you feel ready, close your eyes and begin to breathe very slowly, very gently. Pay close attention to your breathing. Ponder for a moment how grateful you are for breath. Acknowledge that the very breath you are breathing could have been breathed by your great-great-great grandfather three centuries ago, by a Buddhist monk in ancient Tibet, by your mother who lives 500 miles away, or by you three weeks ago.*

*So now, while whispering a prayer of gratitude for the gifts of air, draw in a huge breath. Move this breath through the crown of your head, and send it up toward the heavens while imagining this breath being received as a gift to the Creator for your gratitude. Repeat this action with a second breath. This time, after offering your breath to the Creator, draw from the Creator a gift of Light. In your mind's eye, see or sense the Light coming down toward you. Allow the Light to enter the crown of your head. Gently guide this gift through your body. When it reaches your feet, move the Light out the soles of your feet.*

*Take a third deep breath. This time, bring the Light into the centre of your chest. Allow it to form into a colored ball. Sense the ball getting bigger and bigger, its color brighter and brighter. Now gently move the Light from your body into the space surrounding you. Send the light one arm's length above, beneath, in front, and behind you. Spend a few moments holding this precious gift within and around you, and then return to the six-foot outline of your physical body.*

Now, using colored chalk pastels draw your spiritual self onto the outline you have just completed. Draw what you experienced and perhaps witnessed in your mind's eye. Also draw what you know, or sense your Divine Light, your Spiritual Essence looks like. It might be helpful to think of how your Spiritual Essence would appear to someone with clairvoyant vision. Make a visual representation of what this person would see.

When you have completed this activity, journal the experience and any insights that you gained as you were doing the activity, as well as any awareness that surfaced following its completion. After you have completed the initial journal entry, reflect on the following questions: What color did you choose for the formation of your physical outline? What color or colors did you see or sense being directed to you? Did you draw colored Light energy coming into your crown and moving all the way through your body? Did you draw colored Light energy moving out of your hands and out the soles of your feet?

We are delicate and intricate systems of colored energy. It is impossible to speak with any accuracy about our spiritual essence without an understanding of energy and how energy moves through the human body and through all of creation.

Practice feeling your spiritual essence. Place your hands about four inches apart and gently bring them back together until they are nearly touching. Do this a few times. Pay attention to any sensations you might have, to anything that might be moving from your fingers. What did you sense? Did you feel heat, tingling, or a sensation of having magnets between your hands? Did you see anything? Did you notice anything that looked like smoke or lights coming from your fingertips or the centre of your palms? Did you see any colors?

Note in your journal what you experienced. Describe your perceptions and insights. The energy you sensed and the colors you saw are significant because they indicate much about you and about your spiritual strengths at this time. I introduce colors and their associated meanings in the following chapter, where I will invite you to review the work you have just completed to gain further insights into your choices of colors.

I first drew a life-size representation of my spiritual self while I attended a therapeutic art session with Patrick Yesh, owner of *Art, Heart, and Soul*.[2] When I returned from his Soulful Art workshop I hung the image in my office. For weeks this visual depiction of my spiritual essence filled my space and penetrated my awareness. Like a mirror, it reflected what I really needed to pay attention to. It clearly portrayed that the changes and shifts that had taken place within me were now being radiated outward. This self-portrait was chiding me that it was time to show the world my true colors.

Some time later I led a similar art activity for a group of 13 counselors to whom I was teaching ways to work more effectively with the soul-pain experiences of others. It was awesome to spend an entire weekend with the spiritual reflections of these 13 glorious beings hanging in the hall-ways, as though in support of the work we were doing. I encourage you to hang the depiction of your radiant essence, and I highly recommend that you repeat this activity with colleagues, and those to whom you provide services and assistance. It is a most empowering activity. Although I have also done this activity using smaller sheets of paper because of the numbers and time or space requirements, I suggest, if it is at all possible, that you use the six-foot sheets. There is magic in seeing a full-blown image of your energetic, radiant essence, your spiritual essence in all its glorious brilliance.

Einstein stated, "All is energy."[3] Things look solid because most people's nervous systems do not currently have the capacity to allow the sensory organs to interpret the rapid movement of most energy vibrations. Yet energy vibrations in the human body are easily measured, including the pattern and rate of the heart, brain, and muscles, and in ever-increasing numbers people are sensing energy around them and are feeling and seeing the energy that extends beyond themselves and others.

Does the picture you just designed of your spiritual essence depict the energy that is moving from you? The energy moving beyond us is referred to as the *human aura* or the *human energy field*. Did you draw your aura? Does your aura completely surround you? Does color completely fill your aura? Do you want to go back and extend your aura, fill it, or brighten its color? Do so if you wish.

If you are not familiar with energy and how energy flows through the human body and radiates from it, ask a partner to do the following exercise with you.

While standing behind your partner and keeping your palms three to four inches from his or her back, and beginning at the head, gently move your hands downward toward your partner's waist. Then return your hands to the top of his or her head and repeat the downward strokes four or five times. Share experiences, and then invite your partner to do the same for you. Once again, share what you both experienced.

Did you "feel" the energy being radiated? Did you see anything, any color? What did you experience when the other was moving energy down your back? Did the experience give you a stronger sense of the realness of energy and energy vibrations?

Not only are we made of energy, but "All" is energy. Although most people are not completely conscious of it, energy waves are all around us. Think of the sounds and sights which animals such as dogs and deer see and hear, which we do not. Think of some of the energy waves that make our lives more comfortable. Think of microwaves and radio and television waves. Think of the energy vibrations rising from the Earth on a hot summer day.

The ancients taught that all was held together by Grandmother Spider's gigantic web and that tugging on any aspect of the web affected the entire web. Their teaching was of a holographic universe, a teaching that is now gathering considerable empirical support.

In *The Field*, Lynne McTaggart[4] reviewed well-designed research from respected scientists from various disciplines and from around the world that demonstrated the validity of the energy field theory and therefore supported our holographic nature as human beings. She stated:

> What they have discovered is nothing less than astonishing. At our most elemental, we are not a chemical reaction, but an energetic charge. Human beings and all living things are a coalescence of energy in a field of energy connected to every other thing in the world. This pulsating energy field is the central engine of our being and our consciousness, the alpha and the omega of our existence. (P. xiii)

A leading scientist and a supporter of the work of other field-theory researchers is Ed Mitchell. Mitchell's need to discover the deeper truths about the universe and humankind's connection to the universe began on his Apollo 14 return flight from the moon. As he stared out the window at the "all-encompassing entity," he experienced "a feeling of connectedness, as though all the planets and all the people of all time were attached by some invisible web."[5]

In the 1940s and 1950s neurophysiologist Karl Pribram from Stanford University and University of London physicist David Bohm introduced holographic theory into Western scientific thought. In his book *The Holographic Universe*,[6] Michael Talbot explained that holographic theory suggests that everything in the universe is interrelated. Within a hologram, every aspect of the whole is contained within every part, and any part can reproduce the whole.

Holographic theory is not new; it has ancient roots. It has been a basic teaching of spiritual masters from various cultures and times. Many healing strategies that have their origins in practices of long ago are based upon this theory. Iridology and reflexology, for example, although reintroduced in our times, actually flow from healing techniques that originated centuries ago. In iridology, every organ of the human body is represented within the iris of the eye. In reflexology every organ of the human body is represented on the sole of the foot. These and other practices based upon knowledge of the hologram acknowledge that each representation of the physical body contains cellular memory of all that has influenced and is currently influencing the particular physical organ being affected and treated. These practices are based upon the philosophy that the spiritual energies consist of and are influenced by what is taking place in the physical, emotional, mental, social, environmental, universal, and cosmic realities of the individual being treated.

Take a moment. Take a couple of markers and draw an iceberg floating in the water.

Water in a dream or in art often symbolizes spiritual consciousness. As you read the following, reflect on the iceberg you just drew. How much of it is within the level of your conscious awareness? How much is still beneath the surface?

When the universe is envisioned from the perspective of holographic theory, "all that unfolds before your eyes is merely an external, fragmentary manifestation of an underlying unbroken wholeness."[7] What unfolds before us is the tip of the iceberg. All that unfolds before us is the explicit order. The explicit order is that which we see, taste, touch, and feel in our three-dimensional reality.

The implicit order is the base of the iceberg. It is the enfolding of our three-dimensional reality. The implicit order is the unbroken wholeness of all that exists beyond the tangible world. The enfolded, implicit order is "the subtle and universal reservoir of all life, the wellspring of all possibilities, and the source of all meaning."[8]

The more we understand energy and how energy works, the more we comprehend holographic theory. The more we comprehend holographic theory, the more we understand our spiritual self. All radiates energy vibrations. Any movement within any aspect of any of the dimensions of a holographic universe sets up a series of vibrations that resonates throughout each of the other dimensions, and ultimately returns to the source. All influences and affects All. All is influenced by and affected by All.

The following **art activity** will advance your awareness of these concepts. To complete the activity, you will require a piece of regular-sized drawing paper, a marker, and a variety of chalk pastels.

Using a marker, the color of your choice, draw the shape of a gingerbread person. Using chalk pastels, surround the shape with three separate layers—auras—drawn as though they were vibratory. The one closest to the body represents the energy emitted from your physical body; color it red. The next represents the energy of your mental body; color it orange. Color the third yellow; it represents the energy of your emotional body. Draw the layers to represent waves of various frequencies that indicate their energy vibrations. Now surround the gingerbread shape and its aura with five more colored layers, each of which is also drawn in wavelike patterns. The layer closest to the emotional layer depicts social relationships; color it green. The next represents culture; color it turquoise. The next represents the natural environment; color it blue. Color the next layer indigo or magenta; it represents the universe. The next represents the cosmos; color this layer violet or purple. To complete the picture, draw a further layer. Do not make this layer solid as the others, but leave even spaces between the spaces of solidness to indicate continuousness, openness, an inability to be contained, limitlessness. Color this layer platinum. It represents the Creative Force, Creator, God, or whatever name you call this limitless energy.

Using a platinum-colored chalk pastel spread a stream of platinum light down from the platinum layer into each of the other layers. Allow some of the color to infiltrate each layer. Move the platinum color down to the figure. Allow the color to blend into the crown of the head, through the entire body, and out the soles of the feet. With gentle sweeps, blend some of the platinum color, which is now flowing out the soles of the feet, into each of the layers beneath the feet. Allow the color to move downward as well as horizontally. Repeat the process using each of the other colors as well, gently stroking through each color in a bidirectional way. Make sure that the colors of each layer flow into and blend throughout each of the others.

Note this experience in your journal. Did this art activity help you to more clearly know the meaning of oneness, the meaning of being "One with the Great All"? Did the exercise help you to know more fully that everything, every aspect of creation, including each of us, is a part of a great and magnificent web, held together by Divine Energy? Did the activity help you to understand that, although Divine Energy exists in all things, there is still an aspect of the Divine that is outside of, yet connected to and influencing the *All*?

Did the artwork help you to more adequately acknowledge your holistic nature and your place in a holistic universe? Did it help you to more fully recognize that what is going on for us physically, mentally, and emotionally impacts each of the other aspects of our being and, consequently, the *All*? Did you gain new awareness of the interrelationship and interdependence of these aspects with the social, cultural, and natural environments, as well as with the universe and the cosmos? Did you gain a greater understanding of how and why we are affected by the phases of the moon, the constellations, and other astrological influences?

Return to the drawing of your *Divine Connection* that you did in a previous chapter. Now that you have completed the above activity, do you notice anything in that previous piece that had not drawn your attention earlier? Reread the journal entry that you made after completing that activity. Examine again your soul's response, your gut instinct as you first saw that drawing. Do your initial responses from that activity speak louder now? Do you see any parallels between what you drew then and the last activity? Have the two activities helped to heighten your awareness of yourself as a spiritual being?

What has been reinforced in your artwork is the teaching of all Spiritual Masters. As though with one voice they reiterate, "We are one with the Divine; we are one with the Divine Force in All. The Divine Force flows through us, flows through All!" Your art activity and the teachings of the Masters describe our true nature, a nature now supported not only by philosophers, but by scientists and researchers as well.

We are like a gigantic aqueduct with an incredible capacity for volume and velocity. Our opening to the Divine, our "pipe," can be wide and open to receiving and to giving love or it can be narrow with corrosions, corrosions of fear and regret, similar to a sclerotic artery narrowed by plaque.

Corrosion in our spiritual pipe blocks our progress. When we truly know of our Sacred Union, fear no longer controls us. Fear is always about separation. The more we feel separate and apart from the Divine and from the Divine Energy in All, the less we trust the universal order. The less we trust the universal order, the less able we are to take risk. The less able we are to risk, the less able we are to move our lives in the direction of our soul's purpose.

We have been told that we are separate, that we are not one with our Creator, and in response we shrivel and rust. We have been taught that we are unworthy of such a connection. We have been made to believe that we require an intermediary, an elder, a priest, a teacher, a savior to intercede on our behalf. Dogmatic teachings of the last centuries have caused us to deny our Sacred Oneness. We have been taught to fear practices that acknowledge this ancient wisdom—the wisdom that helps to increase our ability to draw the Connecting Force through us. Yet, this is brokenness. It is our separation and our feelings of being disconnected and apart that keep us from knowing and experiencing our own Divine Essence.

Our Divine Essence is our Light. It is the energy we emit. It is the Divine Force that flows to us and through us and that radiates from us. Each of us is a channel for Divine Light. The more we open to allow the Divine Light to fill our being, the more the flow increases. The more the flow increases the greater our capacity to radiate this Light beyond. The more we radiate our Light beyond, the broader our channel for receiving becomes.

Flushing our aqueduct of fears increases its diameter and permits immense increases in both volume and velocity. An increased volume and velocity of Divine Force flowing through us directly increases our power to tap into the All and to use the power of the All to effect changes in every aspect of our All-ness. The fewer the fears of our Divine Connectedness, the greater is our capacity to draw from the ever-abundant stream. The more we draw in, the greater and more rapid the flow in response to the demand.

This notion is basic to drawing in abundant energy in its various forms and for various purposes, including healing. In all forms of energy healing, a healer learns to open wide his or her channel to draw in greater amounts of Divine Light. This Light is then sent through the mind, the heart, and the hands of the healer to the person requesting healing.

As you reflect on the drawing you just completed, notice the size of the opening that moves through the figure you created. If you choose, take the chalk pastels and widen the main energy channel to allow a greater amount of Divine Light to flow through you. Remember, externalizing in any form the desires of the heart and soul make them more solid in this dimension. Recall also that although our creative work reflects our souls' energy as it is currently, we can also use artwork to give our souls images of the directions in which we choose to move. In this way externalizing is similar to making a list. When I make a list in the morning, I almost always accomplish what

I set out to complete during that day. When I do not, I often find myself thinking at the end of the day of the many small tasks I have left undone (and I therefore have to make a list before I can sleep!).

If you have chosen to heal at a soul level, it is necessary to open and maintain a wide channel for receiving and sending Divine Energy. As the following model depicts, Divine Energy flows from the Divine Source through every aspect of our holographic nature. Our core is Divine, and it radiates Divine Energy. Divine Energy flows to us and from us. Every aspect of our holistic nature is permeated and influenced by the Divine energy

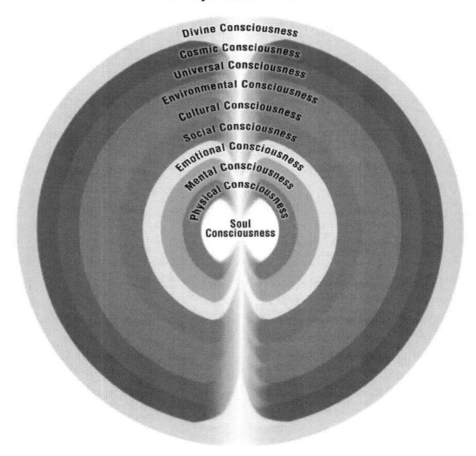

## Our Spiritual Nature

Divine Consciousness
Cosmic Consciousness
Universal Consciousness
Environmental Consciousness
Cultural Consciousness
Social Consciousness
Emotional Consciousness
Mental Consciousness
Physical Consciousness
Soul Consciousness

Copyright Jane A. Simington, Ph.D. (2003).

flowing to us and is permeated and influenced by the Divine energy flowing from us. We are a result of the greater whole, and the greater whole is a result of us. All aspects are interrelated; every aspect affects every other aspect. When any aspect wanes, every other aspect also wanes. Our physical being, for example, is influenced by every dimension of the All and influences every other dimension of the All. Each of our physical responses, including every look we give, every sound we make, and every action we perform, impacts the All. Consciousness of each and every one of these experiences is stored in every aspect of our wholeness. Our thoughts, our feelings, our interactions in relationships, and environmental influences, including those of the larger universe, each affect every aspect of the All. When our thoughts and feelings are those that move us forward, every aspect of the All moves forward. When they are less than positive, every aspect of the All is thus affected.

The beliefs that we hold based upon our social and cultural values, including our inclusion and exclusion practices, influence every aspect of our being and every aspect of the All. Acts of reverence and respect positively affect us individually, socially, culturally, and environmentally. Acts of irreverence and disrespect affect us and our social, cultural, natural, and universal environments in ways that are less than positive. All acts mirror our Light, our aura, our soul's energy to the entire universe. We are a product of energetic colored light that reveals for All each and every interrelated interaction within and between the physical, mental, emotional, social, cultural, natural, universal, and cosmic aspects of our being.

To be truly free, we must comprehend our holographic relationship, for in a holographic universe there is no such thing as a "me" and a "not me." When we understand this, we recognize that to help personally is to help all of humanity, and the entire cosmos.

---

# CHAPTER 7

# ACHIEVING WHOLENESS

> *Understand that thou art another world in little,*
> *and hast within thee the Sun and the Moon, and also the stars.*
>
> Origen of Alexandria

We are beings of color and sound. Our bodies draw various frequencies of colored light and sound. We reverberate with colored light and sound, and we radiate colored light and sound. Having knowledge of color and sound and understanding how they manifest within the human body and within our world helps immensely to know how to apply the information so that color and sound can once again, as in ancient times, be used for healing purposes.

As depicted in the diagram of *Our Spiritual Nature*, energy flows to us from the Divine Source and from that source passes through each aspect of our holographic being. Whirling centers within our energetic bodies, known as *chakras*, reduce the energy from the higher frequencies to levels with which we are able to resonate. Each of these whirling centers radiates one of the rainbow colors.

Knowledge of the chakras and of how to do healing work based upon this information is fundamental to an understanding of many of the mythical and spiritual practices that are once again becoming a part of our culture, having returned to us from other parts of the world and other belief systems. An understanding of how to apply these ancient teachings is an essential component of the application of holistic methods of healing. Although much of what is written about the chakras is presented from an

Eastern philosophical point of view, astrologers, alchemists, healers, and shamans in numerous other cultures and traditions have known of these spiritual centers and have used this knowledge in healing practices.

The use of color as therapy, the use of crystals (because of their color and sound frequencies), and the use of music in therapy makes sense when we recognize that each of the whirling chakra centers resonates with a note on the musical scale, the frequency of which matches the vibration of its color.

The note C on the musical scale and the color red resonate within the first energy center, the root chakra, located in the center of the perineum. Its element is Earth, and although astrologers differ on which planets govern which chakras, some believe that the planet Saturn governs the root chakra. Wherever we find Saturn in the horoscope, we usually find the limitations and blockages chosen to be worked on as part of this life's mission. Some astrologers, who continue to recognize Pluto as a planet, associate Pluto with transformation and with the root chakra. The root chakra draws energy to it in a frequency required to keep us connected to the Earth and to help us move through the blockages and thus transform. We are in this dimension to do good deeds, deeds aimed at advancing all of humankind. We are unable to do so unless we are really grounded in the physical realities. We need to be always advancing the spiritual aspects of our nature, but if we focus only on the spiritual, we have little success in moving good works forward in this dimension. Most of us, in this lifetime and on this dimension, are meant to be prayerful doers. When the root chakra is fully functioning, we know of our place in this world. We are in awe of this and feel connected to all that has been created.

The next five chakras each have an anterior as well as a posterior opening. The posterior opening for each of chakras two, three, four, and five are located along the spinal column, directly across from their anterior partner. The posterior opening for chakra six is located at the back of the head directly across from the brow, where the anterior opening of chakra six is located.

The second chakra is located just above the pubic bone and is the center of sexuality and reproduction. Because we create—give life to—much more than children, this centre is associated with reproduction and birthing in its many forms, including the development and expansion of our many gifts and talents.

Water is the element associated with birth and birthing, a connection garnered from the nurturing and support of life given by the uterine waters. Because of this connection, water is the element most often associated with this chakra.

The second chakra is governed by Jupiter, the planet of expansion and opportunity, and thus is also known as the centre of abundance, for as we creatively bring to life our talents and send our gifts out to the world, abundance returns to us. The color most often associated with abundance and creativity and with the second chakra is orange. Both the color orange and the second chakra resonate to the musical note D.

This center reflects our ability to become who we are meant to be and to allow those aspects of our being to resonate with the collective. The challenge in keeping this center functioning fully is to keep our connection to the Great All as open as possible. To do so, we must constantly draw in energy that can assist us in developing all of our talents and abilities to their fullest and to then find ways to move our fully developed gifts out into the world for the good of All. "I develop *all* of my talents and creative abilities in the most successful and abundant ways for the good of all" is a powerful affirmation that you might like to use to keep this chakra functioning fully and to thus move your life forward.

The third chakra is located in the solar plexus. This center reflects and responds to the emotional aspects of ourselves and the emotional energies surrounding us. This is why this energy centre is often referred to as the center of courage and risk taking. Once we know what we are good at, which is the gift we gained from the second chakra, we must risk stepping out in courage to share our gifts with the world. This is not always an easy task, but only through risk-taking can we achieve success, the gift of the third chakra. We feel acceptance and rejection in this center and because of this, risk taking can be difficult. If our need to be approved of and accepted is too great, we may resist taking the risks needed to move our life's purpose forward for fear of disapproval or rejection.

This chakra is ruled by Mars, the planet of fire. In its less refined state, the energy of Mars relates to anger and aggression. As we master the "fire in our belly," anger and aggression burn away, allowing us to more readily express strength and assertiveness. In claiming and voicing our personal power, we automatically propel our life and our life's work forward. We place faith in our own decisions and rely less on the opinions and approval of others.

Yellow, the color of courage, and the musical note E resonate with this, the third energy centre. Meditation on its color and sound helps to harness the positive manifestations of this chakra. Affirming the release of difficult emotions and focusing on moving life forward also strengthens this centre. An affirmation to enhance the third chakra and move the energy toward the fourth chakra is "As I release the past, I move forward with joy and confidence."

The fourth chakra, the heart chakra, is located in the center of the sternum, between the breasts. It is the center of love and compassion. Opening this chakra to its fullest depends on our God-love connection to self and all. Chanting words and phrases that carry the pitch of the musical note F, the sound associated with this centre, and doing breath meditations (air being the element of this centre), are time honored ways of strengthening the human potential for love and compassion.

The heart center reflects and draws to itself green, the color frequently associated with love and hope. It is the center from which we project love inwardly to self and outwardly to others. It is also, however, the center where we hold unresolved issues related to self-love and love for others. As this center opens even wider, it reflects and draws to itself the color of rose-pink. The color rose is associated with compassion, a higher degree of love. Compassion is often referred to as love without hooks, meaning that we love others with no expectations; to love without expectations means to love without conditions. This is why rose quartz crystals are often used in healing when there is a great need for self-love and compassion.

As the heart center expands and opens to the third layer, it radiates and draws to itself chartreuse, a lime-green color. The color chartreuse reminds us to love because we know ourselves and others as spiritual beings on a human journey and to love and respect each situation and circumstance despite outward appearances. When the heart centre opens to the fourth layer, it draws to itself and radiates a gold color. Many spiritual practices teach that the seed of the soul is planted behind the heart chakra and that the door to the soul opens to the color gold.

Although a major discussion of the relationship between the planets and the chakras is beyond the scope of this book, it is interesting to know that whereas many astrologers associate Venus, the planet of love, with this chakra, others identify the sun as being the most powerful source of influence on this chakra. Who among us does not find it easier to feel loving and lovable on a sun-infused day?

The color gold is in many traditions, both past and present, associated with the masculine aspect of Divine Energy. For this reason many cultures have found the sun a fitting symbol of the Divine. Examine a child's drawings. You will rarely find one that does not include the sun. Is this revealing an innate knowing? Examine your own artwork. Have you included a sun or a sun symbol in any or all of the work that you have recently completed? Does this perhaps indicate that your soul is encouraging you to reconnect and possibly enhance the flow of this aspect of Divine Energy into your life? Has your artwork included pictures of sunflowers? Many cultures use sunflowers and marigolds to symbolize the soul, for these flowers rotate their heads to follow every movement of the "sun god." If your artwork includes these symbols, what messages might they be revealing to you?

The fifth chakra is in the throat. Its color is blue; its element is ether—the atmosphere, the heavens. It resonates to the musical note G. It is the center of knowledge, the center for knowing spiritual truth, which includes knowing who we really are and knowing of our connection to the larger universe.

Mercury is the planet coupled with the fifth chakra. Mercury is the planet associated with communication. To open this chakra and keep it functioning well, we must not only know the spiritual truths, but also communicate them to others.

The sixth chakra draws and reflects the color indigo or magenta. It resonates to the note A. This center is often referred to as the third eye. It is located in the center of the forehead, just above the eyes. It is the center of insight and intuition. The energy in this center corresponds in a holographic way to the energy of the greater universe. As this centre opens, there is a realization of our personal divinity, which displays in meditation and in our art forms as the five-pointed star. As this centre opens, we connect with our expanded senses, including clairvoyance and clairaudience. This is why this centre is acknowledged as the center for understanding more fully how to apply spiritual truths for self-healing and the healing of others.

The seventh chakra is known as the crown chakra. It exists at the top of the head, many believe at the place of the "soft spot" on the skull in infancy. The crown chakra opens into many chakras, each capable of drawing in higher frequencies of energy as we develop spiritually. It connects us to the energy of the higher dimensions. This chakra rules our personal contact with the "God-consciousness" and is represented in Eastern philosophies by the lotus with a thousand petals. This chakra draws and reflects violet hues of various degrees and frequencies. The lowest of the crown chakras resonates with the musical note B. Higher openings of this chakra resonate with musical notes generally not audible to most human ears, although it is important to acknowledge that many on this planet are once again beginning to hear, if only for seconds, the glorious music known as the song of the universe. I ponder this awareness each time I view music notes on a collage or other pieces of someone's artwork. I was gifted to hear this music, albeit for a brief second, a number of years ago during an evening meditation within the ancient stone circle of Stonehenge.

As Origen of Alexandria[1] stated, there is truly within us another world in little, a world containing the sun, the moon, the stars, the rainbow, and the song of the universe.

Reexamine all of your artwork. Examine each piece for the colors you used. Be sure to also look at the background color of the paper you chose for your collage or drawing. What color or colors did you use the most? Is this because you have a great need for the frequencies of that color in your life right now and you are drawing it to you? Or is it because you have a lot of that color and are now able to give some back to the holographic universe?

Have you used a lot of red? Red is the color of blood and often represents physical health and vitality. Are you being reminded to honor your physical body, your physical health? Are you being reminded to more fully express your spirituality in a physical and tangible way? Are you being asked to be more rooted and grounded to really make your life work? On the Great Medicine Wheels around the world, red is the color most frequently placed in the South. It is there to remind us that we must honor the physical body, for it houses Spirit. It is also the color frequently associated with learning to trust, for even though we are in physical form, we are being guided and supported by the Spirit Worlds. What insights can you glean as you ponder these teachings and as you once again reflect on your artwork?

When children are asked to pick a favorite color, many pick red. I believe that is because they require a lot of this color to become more fused and grounded in their physicality. I have witnessed the spirit of a child moving in and out of her physical body. When that happened, I wondered if that little spirit was trying to decide whether she should remain in this physical expression.

If you have used a lot of red, do you also need the energy of this frequency to connect more completely to your physicality and to this dimension? The color red often appears in our artwork, in our decorating schemes, and even in the clothing we choose when we are being invited to honor the Earth in more sacred ways, to know the Earth as a living being, as our true Mother, to stand in awe of all the life She supports, and, indeed, to be in awe of all that has been created.

Red is also the color associated with fire. Fire warms; fire burns away. Ponder this use of fire in your physical and spiritual life. What needs warming? What requires burning so that newness can grow?

Have you used a lot of orange? Are you being asked to be more creative? Are you being reminded to develop and share your gifts and abilities? The second chakra, the one that resonates with orange, is also the chakra of abundance. Are you using your talents in the most abundant ways, or do you need the energy frequencies of orange to assist in drawing abundance to you?

The third chakra resonates with the color yellow and is the centre of success and risk-taking. Have you used a lot of yellow? On the Great Medicine Wheels, yellow is associated with the East, the place of new beginnings. The color is therefore also the color of new beginnings, of clarity and illumination. Are you being asked to be courageous in your risk-taking behaviors to be able to move your life forward?

Green flows from the heart centre, and, as I stated earlier, it appears with spiritual expansion layers of rose-pink, chartreuse, and gold. These colors support us in becoming more loving toward ourselves; they assist us in developing greater compassion for others and for all other aspects of creation. Have you used these colors? What messages are you being given? Do you need one or more of these colors right now, or are you radiating that color from you so that others may pick up that energy?

Blue, the color of the throat chakra, is the color of truth and knowledge. Have you used an abundance of that color? Is there a need to advance in your attainment of spiritual knowledge? Because this is also the centre of communicating truth, you might also ask yourself if it is time to share that knowledge. Blue is also the color of water and is used in the rituals of most traditions to signify healing, cleansing, and rebirth. Many of the great Medicine Wheels place blue in the West, the place of healing. This is why the west and the color blue are also often associated with a healer.

If you have used a lot of blue you might want to ponder your own need to advance along your healing journey. Or you may want to examine your potential as a healer.

Turquoise blue is the color of protection. As we step forward in sharing spiritual truths, we often sense an increased need for spiritual protection. The energy of turquoise blue can assist in developing this form of protection. This is why many healers wear turquoise and silver jewelry.

Clairvoyant healers teach that a new energy centre is opening. The color of this chakra is turquoise. Its element is silver. Many spiritual teachers associate the moon with this centre. It is located on the sternum, between the heart and the throat chakra. Its purpose is to help us to communicate more effectively, with assistance available from the higher spiritual realms. This positive and loving energy is being made available to humankind, helping us to move in a peaceful, loving, and protected way through the Earth-changes. Earth-changes, predicted in the sacred teachings of cultures from various parts of the world, are said to help bring closure to the energies associated with the Age of Pisces and to help usher in the higher frequencies associated with the Age of Aquarius. These changes are already occurring, and many believe they are to be complete between the years 2012 and 2015.

In my mentoring programs I have noticed that as people recognize their intuitive and healing powers, they also begin to display in their artwork the moon and the colors silver and turquoise, all of which are associated with the Divine Feminine. Examine your artwork. Have you used a lot of turquoise, silver, the moon or crescent shapes?

If turquoise stones have been appearing in your life or if a lot of that color is appearing in your artwork, you might like to ponder some of these teachings. You might also wish to ponder your cosmic connections and the role that you are to play in assisting the Earth's people through the changes.

Healers who are familiar with the qualities of crystals and gems often use stones in the colors of the chakras to stimulate the energy and assist in healing the associated chakra. Have gems or crystals or the color of one or more of the chakras become significant to you? If so, what might that indicate?

Indigo is the color most often associated with the third eye. Indigo is usually portrayed on color wheels as a blue-purple. I personally always see this color as more of a deep magenta than indigo, and because of this I wonder whether the frequency now required by this chakra has increased. Did you use a lot of either indigo or magenta in your artwork? If so, are you being asked to expand your insights, your awareness, your consciousness, and perhaps to use your intuitive gifts for healing purposes?

Have you discovered an abundance of violet and purple colors in your life? Are you being encouraged to expand as a spiritual being? Are you investing much energy at this time in trying to find answers to the spiritual questions in your life? Are you attempting to come to know more fully who you really are as a spiritual being?

In this system of color sources and the identification of their accompanying meanings, purple hues are most often associated with the spiritual aspects of a human being. Many, however, associate white with spiritual energies. It is valuable to acknowledge that white is the combination of the rainbow colors. If you were to spin the entire rainbow, you would get white. What a wonderful indication of wholeness! On the Great Medicine Wheels of the world, the color white is placed in the North, the place of the ancestor, the white buffalo, and the leader. Identify how you have used white in your art pieces. Have you seen white light pouring into you during a guided meditation? What is the significance of this?

Many believe that the color black is the mass of all color, but black is actually an absence of color. Although black does not appear as a chakra color, it is the color sometimes placed in the West on the Great Medicine Wheels. This is because the West is the place of healing. Black can remind us to go into the void, like a bear goes into its cave. During our time of hibernation we can come to know more fully our own truth. Going into the void, into the "dark night of the soul," is an essential part of the spiritual journey. If you have been drawn to wear or use in other ways a lot of black recently, are you being asked to go into the stillness of your own soul, there to discern your own truth? Although many in Caucasian cultures have been taught that black is less than positive, and although it certainly can reflect less than positive aspects of our nature, people from other cultures, specifically those from the Blackfoot tribes of North America and people from Guatemala, view black as a sacred color. It is the color that they use most frequently in their art and design work.

People raised in Christian traditions will perhaps recognize the association between the chakra colors, the characteristics ascribed to them, and the "gifts of the Spirit." The gifts of the Spirit are introduced to children when they are confirmed into their faith tradition. Starting at the crown chakra and moving toward the root chakra, the gifts are wisdom, understanding, knowledge, compassion, courage, creativity, and awe of all that has been created. During the Sacrament of Confirmation the bishop seals these gifts into the head—the crown chakra. The candidate is reminded to develop these gifts and to use them to make the world a better place. Each of these gifts has a symbol. During an attunement with a spiritual healing practice such as Reiki, the master performs a similar practice in which the sacred symbols of healing are placed within the crown chakra of the apprentice.

The similarities in these initiation practices point to the Christian fathers' overlay of traditional cultural practices with ceremonies of the new religion. It speaks to their recognition of the spiritual significance of the chakras and of the deep spiritual truths contained within the chakras and reflected from them.

Examine your previous artwork for symbols. You might be surprised at how many appear. We generally do not acknowledge the symbolic language of our soul, yet symbols are all around us. Look for the Christian symbols; look for symbols of Reiki and other healing traditions; look for symbols associated with each of the chakras as depicted in Eastern traditions and philosophies. Examine your artwork for the symbols associated with the zodiac, the planets, the sun, the moon, and the elements. You can increase your familiarity with them by checking associated websites or symbol books. Note any similarities among the symbols of different traditions and practices. What might the symbols that appear in your particular artwork be communicating?

Some Indigenous peoples associate a totem animal with each of the spiritual centers. These totems, or power animals, often appear in art forms, in dreams, or during a guided imagery even to those who are not, in this incarnation, of Indigenous background.

If animals appear in your artwork, you will find it valuable to examine the particular characteristics of those animals and determine how this applies to your life. Ted Andrew's book *Animal Speak*[2] is an excellent resource to enhance your learning about animals and the gifts that these totems bring into our lives.

Animals associated with the Eastern zodiac also surface in artwork as well as in dreams. Examine your creative endeavors. If the rat, ox, tiger, rabbit, dragon, snake, horse, sheep, monkey, rooster, dog, or pig, appear, glean information from both Eastern and Western sources on the meanings associated with that particular animal discovery and the influences that it might have on your life. We are often amazed when symbols from other cultures appear in our work, especially when we know little or nothing about that culture. I believe this is evidence of the age and expansiveness of our souls and of the language that soul uses to communicate.

Contemporary literature has also reawakened the ancient teachings that associate each of the chakras with an Archangel. These angels are willing to assist when called upon. They can help the specific energy frequencies required to fully open and keep the associated chakras functioning.

Below is a guided meditation. In this mediation you will call on the Archangels, one by one, to help you focus on the chakra to which they are each assigned.

You might like to read it through once to get a good sense of the content and then ask a trusted friend to read it to you. Find a peaceful place where you will not be disturbed. Taking all the time you need, gently and slowly allow yourself to be guided through the process. When you have completed the meditation, you will find it valuable to remain in silence for a few moments, because, following a meditation, we sometime have beautiful visuals or thoughts that are important to pay attention to.

*Begin by shifting yourself to a place of peace by paying close attention to your breathing. Breathe in and out… in and out… in and out…. As you do, allow yourself to gently and easily begin to relax under the calming effects of your breathing.*

*Draw in a full, deep breath. Gently raise that breath through your crown chakra. Send it high into the universe and then beyond. Imagine sending this breath all the way up to your Creator. Place your breath, containing everything that is no longer working for you, right in your Creator's hand.*

*Now from your Creator receive a powerful gift of healing Light. Bring the gift of Light into the crown of your head. Imagine your crown chakra spinning violet as you pray, "Archangel Jophiel, blaze through me the light of illumination!" Imagine a light, much like a lightning bolt descending from above. Allow it to flash through your entire body. Visualize it moving from you, out the soles of your feet.*

*Focus now on your brow as you pray, "Archangel Raphael, offer assistance as I open to my healing abilities for myself and others!" Imagine the brow chakra spinning vibrantly; as it spins, add colors of indigo or magenta.*

*Next, visualize your throat chakra spinning blue as you pray, "Archangel Michael, act as my protector as I discover truth and communicate this knowledge."*

*Move your focus to your heart centre and pray, "Archangel Chamuel, help me to give and receive love of the highest order!" As you pray, imagine this chakra spinning green, then rose-pink, chartreuse, and gold.*

*Move your awareness to your solar plexus, and spin it a vibrant yellow as you pray, "Archangel Uriel, help me take the risks I need to take. Help me stand in courage as I do so!"*

*Focus now on your pelvic chakra. Visualize it spinning orange as you pray, "Archangel Gabriel, help me develop to the fullest all of my talents and abilities!"*

*As you move your attention to your root chakra, pray, "Archangel Zadkiel, keep me grounded and connected to the Earth. Bring into my life those who need what I have to offer. Bring those who can help move my gifts into the world for the good of all, and in the most abundant way!" Spin the root chakra a vibrant red. Then send the red swirling from you down toward the Earth.*

When you are ready, allow yourself to gently return to the present time and place, and then journal your experience as completely as possible. Note any visuals, any sounds you may have heard. Be sure to note any new awareness that you have gained, for each meditation strengthens your spiritual vibrations and brings advanced understanding of one or more spiritual teachings.

A number of years ago I attended a workshop in which we did various meditations, all with the intention that we would raise the energies of each participant to the point where we would each come to acknowledge ourselves as spiritual beings having a human experience. During the course of the weekend the facilitator referred to the notion that we each have a primary soul color. Although she gave no further information, it was a concept to which my soul wanted me to pay attention. A few months later while doing an early-morning outdoor meditation, I was given affirmation in support of her teaching.

The morning was glorious. The sun had risen to just above the horizon. Gazing into this radiant sight, I began saying my prayers of gratitude for the gifts of the East. I closed my eyes, hoping to capture and maintain, deep within my being, the experience and the golden light. As I did, I witnessed a marvelous and beautiful sight. A woman in a flowing gown came running toward me. Her dress was delicate and soft, yet vibrantly blue. She was surrounded with an aura of green, fringed in a cloud of pink-purple. The colors were electric, the vivacity of which I have not the words to communicate. Long after the vision faded, I lingered, captivated by her smile, the flow of her garments, and the radiance of the colors.

I journal each sacred experience for it helps me to interpret the meaning. However, I felt little need to do so that morning because the message was clear. I knew I had witnessed my very own soul and the colors of its reflection. I am a healer. I am a teacher. These are my gifts. These are my soul's colors. It was again a message that it was time for me to show the world these colors.

The ability to connect with soul colors is not only mine. After leading hundreds of people on guided imageries I have discovered that the first color or colors with which we connect are most often the colors associated with our souls' energies. These colors are reflected to us as a reminder of who we are and of our life's purpose. The reflection of our souls' colors happens in a variety of ways. They appear in our art work, in the clothing we prefer to wear, and in the colors with which we decorate. They show themselves during meditation and visualization, and, as in my case, they were reflected from the sun's light.

A few months after the initial experience of seeing my soul's colors, I was teaching a group of counselors about the power of connecting with the soul of the person we are trying to assist through a difficult experience. I had spoken of the use of creative activities and had discussed some of the symbolism of colors and why we might select a certain color. One young man had been told that his color was red, even though the color he used most frequently in his artwork was blue. I asked the group whether they would all like to be led on a guided visualization to identify their soul's color. They were eager. In an alpha-state group meditation, each entered a deep level of their heart and crossed the threshold into the level of their soul. There they witnessed their own radiance. Each discovered the colors of their essence. Each returned from the experience empowered by the knowing. The young man who had been informed that his color was red discovered deep within his core a very vibrant blue, and, in so doing, he discovered a great truth. He now understood that the truth for his soul lies not without, but within. And of at least equal importance, in discovering his soul's true color, blue, the color of truth and knowledge, he came one step closer to claiming his role as a teacher of spiritual truths.

As we become more aware of ourselves as beings of color and sound, we not only more fully comprehend ourselves as spiritual beings with a mission to accomplish, but we also begin to recognize and apply the healing methods that flow from this knowing. Many are awakening to these ancient truths. This, I believe, is one reason that we are witnessing expansion in therapeutic settings of the use of color and other healing modalities based upon this understanding.

Paying attention to the colors we feel drawn to can suggest a desire for more support for a particular chakra or area of the body. If you are drawn to wear orange, for example, this may be a very creative time in your life. You are perhaps instinctively attracting to yourself the color you need to supplement your second chakra, your center of creativity. If, on the other hand, you have a creative project you would like to begin, but can't seem to get things moving, increasing the color orange in your life can help to propel the project forward. This can happen in many ways, such as adding orange-colored garments to your wardrobe and introducing orange into your decorating scheme.

Color therapy can also be used to supplement other remedies being used to treat physical ailments. Those who recommend color as therapy suggest using the color associated with the chakra that governs the part of the body affected. Some examples include the use of orange to assist in the healing of sexual and urinary elimination problems, yellow for digestive conditions, and green and pink to add support to the heart.

One of the easiest ways to apply color therapy is to set bottles of colored water in a window where the sun will reflect the light from the color onto you. If you want a full-spectrum healing, I suggest using a bottle for each of the rainbow colors and placing them in a window where you will receive the reflection for a good number of hours each day. Adding the frequency of the sound associated with the colors of the chakras on which you are focusing will enhance the healing effects to an even greater degree. Spend some time browsing a favorite bookstore that stocks spiritually focused resources. You will likely find a recording or two with instrumental music designed for this purpose.

Although I stated previously that each chakra resonates to a particular musical note, it is important to acknowledge that all sounds and all types of music affect the colors and the energy of the chakras and of our entire system and therefore, because of our holographic nature, likely the entire cosmos. The frequency of the vibrations can relax or stimulate, promote calm or increase anxiety.

Reflect on the effects of lullabies on infants and children. Ponder how relaxation music and ocean-wave sounds promote peace and relaxation for older and dying persons in long-term and palliative care. Think also of how hard-rock and heavy-metal music might affect our adolescents, whose energy centers are daily filled with enormous degrees of harsh vibrations— vibrations that also often convey in deep subliminal ways less than positive messages about self-worth, human values, and even life itself.

In *The Hidden Messages in Water,* Masaru Emoto[3] described his use of high-speed photography to capture the formation of crystals in frozen water. He discovered that the crystals reveal changes demonstrative of the types of music being directed toward them. He found that water exposed to gentle, peaceful music displays brilliant colorful snowflake patterns. In contrast, water exposed to harsh sounds and negative lyrics form incomplete patterns with dull colors.

As you ponder the numerous possibilities for being affected by sound in less than positive ways, consider also all the ways in which color and music affect our individual lives in positive ways. Many spiritual and religious traditions have taught that everything—the Earth, the entire universe—was created from sound. For centuries, chanting practices built upon this teaching have been used to manifest peace, harmony, and all good things. Around the globe today chanting groups gather with the goal of recreating a world where peaceful vibrations dominate.

Museums are filled with musical artifacts that bear symbols reinforced with the power of tribal and cultural colors. The rhythmic vibrations of humming and song, and the music and sounds of the flute, the drums, and the rattles have been (and continue to be) methods used to heal and guide the soul as it journeys to the spirit world in search of answers. Drumming circles are forming in ever-increasing numbers and in many parts of the world as the call increases to reconnect with the vibrant energy of the Earth Mother's heartbeat.[4] The drum, the flute, and the rattle are reclaiming their places in healing circles, where individuals gather with the hope of receiving healing for body, mind, and spirit and with the hope of reawakening the ancient voice within, the voice that reminds them of their connection to the sacred and to all that is sacred.

Research is now demonstrating in quantifiable ways the effect of rhythm on the human body. The positive results of music therapy, as well as art as therapy, are numerous. These include direct and positive relationships between art and healing and between music and relaxation. They also suggest a positive relationship between music and the stimulation of memories.[5, 6, 7, 8, 9, 10, 11, 12]

We can often recall what age we were, where we were, and even exactly what we were doing when we first heard a particular tune. We are aware of the songs that bring joy-filled memories; we are also aware of songs from our past that bring tears. Music stirs the soul. It opens the chakras. It is a powerful tool for releasing pain-filled memories locked deeply within. Music stimulates stored memories. Once the memories are stimulated, they surface, and they can then be examined and enjoyed or examined, healed, and then released. Healing and releasing difficult memories severs the chains that keep a soul in bondage. Once severed from pain-filled memories, the soul can rapidly take flight into freedom.

Because some of our earliest and deepest memories are those of rhyme, rhythm, music, and song, therapists often purposefully use these powerful strategies to assist another in doing deep healing work, including healing that needs to take place to bring a peaceful closure to relationships when life is ending.

> Song and music have always been a large part of my family celebrations. Vibrations from the strings on the guitar, mandolin, balalaika, and banjo resonate with many family moments of laughter, and times of sorrow. My brother-in-law is a gifted musician. He and my sister spent many hours at my mother's bedside during her final illness, his guitar always in readiness. The two of them and my brother would frequently arrive for an evening of song, even when it was my turn to be our mother's attendant. Songs I had not sung or even heard for decades easily flowed as our memories of earlier times were recollected. Recapturing in music and in song the positive experiences of the life we each had shared with our mother affirmed for her the positive and love-filled contributions she had made. *Down in the Valley, When the Sun in the Morning Peeks over the Hill,* and *There Is a Church in the Valley by the Wildwood* flowed easily. Even though it was July and five months from Christmas, we often ended our 'love songs' to our mother with some of her favorite carols. *Silent Night* was always among them. Mother would smile, relaxing into her memories, there to revisit those previous times in reverie and perhaps in the dreamtime following our evening serenades.
>
> On frequent occasions, other residents in the facility would pull their chairs into Mother's room or the hallway in order to be a part of the "bringing peaceful closure to life" that was taking place. Each of us left every one of these evenings feeling blessed and a little more grateful for love and life. We each knew that every moment of these times together was sacred; and because of the holiness of the experiences, our

lives have been forever altered. The holiness of those sacred moments added an indescribable radiance to the brightness of the light burning deep within the recesses of our individual and collective souls.[13]

# CHAPTER 8

# BEING DEEPLY ROOTED IN THE SACRED

*The spiritual life does not remove us from the world,*
*but leads us deeper into it.*

Henri J. M. Nouwen

I am a storyteller and have been a storyteller for much of my life. A story-teller conveys important truths in his or her life, and by actively engaging the listeners, helps them to identify ways in which the messages can be ap-plied to their own lives. Some years ago the need to honor myself as a sto-ryteller became evident during attendance at an art therapy and imagery class. In one of the activities the participants were asked to connect with their roots, the place where unrecognized truths, sometimes described as shadows, reside. A twisted-haired elder came to guide my journey. Within seconds the facilitator's voice faded, and I became a magnificent, shimmer-ing coniferous tree. The image surprised me. Over the years I have had vi-sions of trees, the standing ones, and of becoming one of them. Lately I have witnessed myself as a gigantic golden spruce—a tree once found on Haida Gwaii, the Queen Charlotte Islands, the place of the Haida people. It was startling to see that in the presence of the twisted-hair elder (the storyteller's guide), I shape-shifted into a tree that portrayed other symbols related to other mythologies. Guiding my travels, the twisted-hair elder asked me to experience roots that extended to the sky, where I became one with the air currents, moving through rock canyons, oceans, and the fiery core of the Earth Mother, ending in a pueblo home.

Visual images and sensations continued to unfold as I frantically attempted to externalize in art form, within the limited time allotted, the experience of the inward journey. Now, years later, I remain in awe, not only of the imagery, but also of my discovery in the art supply box. There I found a medallion-like picture portraying an almost identical resemblance to the twisted-haired elder who had arrived to guide my soul travel. The realness of the experience caused me to ponder anew the power of parallel realities. The journey alongside the twisted-haired elder reminded me of the glorious sage-filled hours I had spent years previously with a shaman teacher.

During those days of learning, as I moved gently in and out of parallel realities, I came to recognize and honor the transformational power of nature's in-between places. One such experience tripped me into acknowledging that I did indeed interact with life other than human and that at some level, and at least for some of the time, I was a part of a reality of which I then knew little.

During a training exercise I was encouraged to walk into a forested area, with the intention that the tree, willing to teach what I was most in need of learning, would be revealed. Being new to Shamanic practices and indeed to anything involving working within the spiritual realms, and seriously doubting my abilities in this area, I expected little of significance to occur. Yet I had not ventured far when I felt strongly drawn toward a particularly large Maple tree. Following the Shaman's direction, I asked permission to enter the tree's space. Sensing not only that I was being given permission, but also that the tree was extending a warm invitation, I placed my arms around its trunk. Closing my eyes and pressing my third eye to its bark, as the Shaman had guided, I asked the tree to reveal its history. The request had barely been formulated when newsreel-like images began to unfold. From directly within its centre, the life story of this gigantic Maple tree replayed. I witnessed a tiny seedling, swept by the wind on a sun-drenched plain, growing amidst purple fireweeds, yellow daisies, and millions of other saplings of similar size and variety. I watched as growth flourished and noted that the forest darkened and dampened in response.

Awareness of the effects of decreased sunlight seemed to shift my experience. No longer a witness, I was now an active participant in the unfolding process, absorbed by and being at one with the gigantic Maple. Golden sunlight streamed through our branches, filled our trunk, poured from our enormous and far-reaching roots. In an electrifying process of gratefulness and love, the Earth received our combined and sun-penetrated energies in exchange for cool and life-sustaining nutrients that flowed upward from a place deep within her core.

Although the entire process took a few moments, the experience was life altering. It shifted my perception from believing that I can experience with only five senses and that I live and work in a three-dimensional reality, to knowing that there is so much more that I can be a part of by simply placing intention in the desired direction.

Placing intention shifts perception. Shifting perception expands the senses; expanded senses are the doorways that allow entry to the spiritual realities.

In *Connecting with Nature,* Michael J. Cohen[1] described 53 senses and explained that they can be further subdivided into the over 100 senses that people who can predict earthquakes feel. Some senses are mysterious to us, but as Albert Einstein said, "The most beautiful experience we can have is the mysterious. It is the fundamental emotion that stands at the cradle of true art and science."[2] It is the source of the sacred and the spiritual.

I believe that the first step toward soulful freedom is to recognize that we have many more capabilities than we recognize and that we are able to perceive much beyond what we normally consider possible. Once we perceive these realities, we have little difficulty working within them. When we are able to work within these realities—realities of the sacred—we are able to touch and administer to the needs of the soul.

Yet we have become passive in using our senses. We have somehow adopted the view that we are the receivers of what we see, what we hear, and what we touch, and that all forms of communication are only one way, solely directed by us and for our purposes. This view of reality is built upon the belief that human beings are sentient and that all else in creation is made solely for the purpose of serving human needs. This perspective has not only helped to put much of life on our planet in a precarious position, but has also led human beings to view themselves as separate and apart rather than as one aspect of an interconnected whole.

Yet recognizing this great and grand connection is essential for advancement along the spiritual path. Many exercises are designed for the purpose of expanding our senses and therefore the perceptions of ourselves and our relationships with all of life. The more we experience these connections, the more we experience the multiplicity of realities that surround us in any given moment in time, and the more we are able to enter, at will, the universes of the sacred, a most essential component to assist another in a truly soulful way. The following **activities** will help you to expand to be able to do so.

For this first activity, begin by finding a peaceful place to sit, outdoors if possible. Take a few moments to still your mind. When you feel ready, make the intention that you will experience going out to greet a sound. To do so, simply pay attention to a sound, preferably a pleasant one. For a few moments, listen to the sound as you normally would. Then shift your experience from receiving the sound to sending your hearing out in greeting and acceptance, as you would invite and welcome a guest. Invite the sound to come into your organs of hearing. Listen intently. Then gently move the sound from your organs of hearing down into your heart. Invite the sound in your heart to swell. Extend the sound from your heart and experience it beginning to penetrate your being. Sense the entireness of the sound in the entireness of your being. Did the activity help to expand your perception and your oneness with what you heard?

Repeat the exercise using your sense of touch. Rather than touching the objects, seek to "experience" them? Be mindful of what it feels like to be consciously aware of a process that usually occurs without conscious control.

Try a second **perception-expanding activity**. This one will help to ground your perceptions in this reality. Ask a companion to assist you during this activity. A large portion of his or her role is to "bear witness" to your experience, so verbalize as much as you are able to about what you sense and experience as you do the activity.

Select a place with trees and vegetation, safe for barefoot walking. Ask your companion to blindfold your eyes. Instruct him or her to guide you toward some plant life. Use various parts of your skin and body parts, your feet, arms, face, and back, to touch a variety of grasses, flowers, weeds, leaves, bark, stones, sand pebbles. Select, as well, some man-made objects. Smell a variety of the grasses, trees, and plants. Pay close attention as you do so. What are your smell experiences? What are your touch experiences? What, for example, does the grass smell like, feel like? Does the feeling on your feet and in your body alter as the length of grass varies? What do flowers feel like? Does your experience of them shift depending on the part of your body touched or doing the touching? What do rocks and sand feel like? Do they have a smell? Does the smell vary from one part of the rock to another part? What does a man-made object smell like? What is the temperature of a rock, of a man-made object? Pay attention to the energy vibrations of each plant and object as you experience them. How does the energy vary from plant to plant and object to object? Do you sense a difference in energy between natural and man-made objects? [3]

Ask your partner to lead you toward a large tree. How close do you have to be before you begin to experience the tree, before you sense its aura, its energy field? Seek permission from the tree to enter its presence. If you sense an invitation, embrace the tree. Ask if it is willing to share its history. Verbalize what you witness, hear, feel, smell, and touch.

When you have completed the activities, offer to bear witness as your partner engages in the process. When you have both concluded the movement portions of the experience, find a comfortable place to sit. Without judgment, and while making a clear intention to let go of any need to question your experiences, record all you perceived.

At any time during the above activities did you feel yourself fusing with the plant or mineral life? Did these experiences increase your sense of connectedness and your sense of oneness with the life forms that surround you? Were you able to experience yourself in a much bigger way within a much bigger whole? Did your experiences of melding with other aspects of creation actually heighten, rather than diminish, your own sense of self? Did the experience move you from a place of belief to a place of increased personal knowing? If so, in what ways?

If you experienced being a part of another life form, being a part of a much bigger whole, did you have an increased personal knowing of the sacredness in all things? The following guided journey will strengthen and solidify that connection. Take turns guiding your partner and having your partner guide you.

*Close your eyes now and make an intention to embark on a soul-connecting and advanced-awareness inner journey. Sit in stillness and allow yourself to feel your soul's energy as it begins to penetrate every aspect of your being. Imagine you are seated in front of a Sacred Fire. You are with many others seated in this Sacred Circle. Drumming reverberates from a distance. You vibrate to the rhythm. Feel each of the percussions penetrate and radiate into every aspect of your being. Sense the firmness of the Earth beneath you. Experience the solidness of the contact between the Earth and your physical body. Become aware that each beat of the drum strengthens this contact. Sense the pulse of the Earth Mother. Allow your heart to beat in tempo with her heartbeat.*

As you begin to feel more and more relaxed and in sync with the Earth's heartbeat, allow yourself to gently drift into a very peaceful state of relaxation. As you do so, slowly become aware of a Tree in the process of developing and unfolding, beginning to emerge directly in front of you. Experience this tree pushing forth from the very core of the Earth Mother.

The growth continues; the results expansive, splendorous.

Expand your senses. Expand them even more.

Move your awareness beneath the soil. Note the massive root system; note how the roots tunnel deeply downward. Sense the relationship between the roots and the energies of the Earth Mother

Gaze towards the heavens. Witness the branches ascending upward, outward. Notice the golden rays of Grandfather Sun. Sense the tingling of the branches as the light penetrates. Acknowledge the movement downward and the receptions of the warmth by the trunk, the roots. Acknowledge the gracious acceptance by the Earth Mother of the gifts of light and energy.

Now, gently move toward the Tree. Touch a lower limb. Acknowledge and return the greeting extended to you, the welcome. Accept the invitation. Become surrounded and warmly absorbed by the Tree. Study the merger of your roots as they penetrate the Earth. Experience the welcoming from the Earth Mother.

Receive the gifts of the Earth Mother; receive the abundance pouring up through your roots.

Move your awareness upward to the very tips of your branches. Note the penetrating golden light and the blue of the Sky as they filter into each leaf. Intuit one more time the exchange of gifts between the Earth and the Sky. Experience yourself in the midst of this exchange process. Joyfully assimilate into this incredible and indescribable union. Be One with it. Sink into the Oneness. Delight in the Oneness. Dissolve into the Oneness. Remember who you really are. Remember your Oneness. Be aware again that there is no separation.

Take all the time you wish, and when you feel ready, step forth from the Tree. Embrace and thank the Tree for the gifts and the teachings you received. Return to your place in the Sacred Circle. Hear again the drumming. Send your love around the Circle. Thank each member of this Sacred Community. Thank the drummers. Thank all who have assisted in the journey. Let them know you will be back soon to share and to receive.

Now become aware of being present in every aspect of your being. Open your eyes and recognize your alertness. Acknowledge how fully alive and energized you feel. Recognize that you have had a magnificent and healing journey, and know *that the positive effects of this experience will continue to be with you for hours, days, weeks, and even years to come—and this will all take place, much to your joy and delight.*

Record in your journal all you experienced; then externalize in an **art form** the tree and perhaps other aspects of your experience. As you record and creatively recreate the experience, address in as much detail as possible what you saw, felt, experienced, heard, sensed. Record the meaning and significance to you of each of the aspects of this journey. Pay special attention to the type of tree you became. Identify the season of this journey. Note whether the tree you became was bearing fresh leaves and flowers of spring, the full-blown splendor of summer, or the colors and fruits of autumn, or whether the tree was barren, as in winter.

It is valuable to note that the season of the tree we visualize or create in artwork tends to represent the spiritual seasons of our life. Spring is a time of new beginnings, summer of fruitfulness, autumn a time to harvest, and winter a time to reflect on where we have been and ponder what seeds we will plant in the coming spring.

Trees in bud often represent new life; many leaves can depict a full life; green leaves suggest abundant growth, and colored leaves a colorful life. There may also be symbolic meanings in the types of trees we witness. Oak trees tend to symbolize strength. Willows represent the wood of love and compassion, for they are able to sway and bend, even in times of great sorrow. Cedar and sage trees suggest cleansing, and when they appear, they may be inviting us to clear away the old so that new shoots can take root. Nut trees depict a time for gathering and fruit-bearing trees generally symbolize abundance. The pine is a symbol for peace and of being in harmony with self and others. The birch depicts truth, and the mountain ash or rowan tree represents protection. Both the birch and rowan trees are reputed to be teachers of lessons to learn to identify deception.

Many of my workshop participants are surprised at how easily and clearly they are able to witness a tree when I lead them on a guided visualization. Many are amazed to view a tree that they have never (in this lifetime) seen. It is always awe inspiring to witness how symbolic language surfaces (and often in the most dramatic ways) when we move into soul work.

During a recent retreat dealing with the relationship between creative expression, art, and spirituality, I invited the participants to draw a tree. One woman's tree creation filled the entire page; each huge swaying branch was covered with brightly colored maple leaves. Rings encircled the trunk, making it appear as the trunk of a palm tree. As we processed the exercise, I commented on how the swaying branches bore maple leaves and the trunk appeared to be that of a palm tree. Astonished at what her art had revealed, the woman told of coming as a young adult from Lebanon to Canada. She married an Ontario-born Canadian and worked hard to blend into Canadian culture. Her roots were in the land of the palms; her productivity, incredible growth, outreach, and brilliance belonged in the land of the maple leaf. Her amazing artwork revealed in symbolic form messages that could be interpreted in ways and at a depth that oral and spoken language could not be.

As you examine the artwork of the tree you have created, ponder the qualities of that particular type of tree. Reflect on how those qualities reflect your life and your spiritual unfolding. After you note your insights, discuss with a trusted friend what teachings this might contain for your life.

Although the meanings contained within some of the images, symbols, and sensations we experience in dreams, guided imagery, and artwork reveal themselves only over time, as we grow and change, there is great value in delving into the symbolism in an effort to discover the messages portrayed. We have become, for the most part, a culture void of any real understanding of symbolic language—of soul language. Reawakening to the metaphors presented can more rapidly propel us forward along our sacred journey—the journey we make in the hope of coming to more fully and completely know and live our true identity.

As we ponder the trees in our artwork or revisit the images we receive in a visualization, it can be soul revealing to know that a tree with branches reaching upward may indicate a desire to reach for things of heaven. A tree with wide branches may suggest a warm and loving personality; a well-shaped tree might indicate a well-ordered personality.[4] A tree's trunk symbolizes its strength. There can also be great value in reflecting on the size of the tree's trunk. Some questions you might ask include, "Is the trunk large enough to support the branches, or is a tiny trunk trying to hold up huge branches? What message does this convey?"

Trees are powerful archetypal symbols. An archetypal symbol is one believed to be a part of the collective consciousness of all humankind. We each have the power to tap into this level of knowing and to draw from it an understanding and a similar interpretation for the meanings associated with the symbol, regardless of our gender, religion, or culture.

Cultures around the world have from early times associated trees with the gods and mystical forces in nature. The ancients worshipped the tree as the *axis mundi*, a symbol for the centre of the universe. Because the tree seemed to join the three realms, the underworld, the Earth plane, and the spirit world, the ancients believed that it was a means by which they could communicate between the realms.

While we were on a pilgrimage to the Mayan temples in Northern Mexico, our guide described the Yaxche trees as sacred to the Maya. He stated that the word *Yaxche* literally means "green tree" in Mayan, but that, at a spiritual level of significance, the word refers to the sacred tree, or *Ceba*. The guide noted that the Yaxche tree also represents paradise and a way to reach paradise. He emphasized that in many tribal cultures the Shaman climbs a symbolic tree to access the spirit world. It is also taught that Mohammed ascended to paradise by means of a tree and that both Jesus and the Buddha rose to heaven along the symbolic center of the world—the tree of life.

In times past, peoples from many cultures believed that gods and spirits dwelt in trees. The sound of wind blowing through a tree's leaves has long been interpreted as the voices of gods and spirits, thus contributing to the spiritual powers of forests and groves. In ancient Egypt the sycamore tree represented rebirth in the afterworld and a reminder to those who had died to ascend from the underworld into the world of the Divine. To this day, sycamore trees can be found in Egyptian burial sites. In Greek mythology, Adonis, the god of vegetation, was born from the trunk of a myrrh tree; Daphne changed into a laurel tree to escape Apollo. The Romans taught that the first people were born of oak trees.[5, 6] The Druids considered the yew tree sacred, a protector of sacred energy, and a guardian of sacred truths. Many of the sacred stone circles and holy wells that I visited on pilgrimage in England were guarded by sacred yew trees. Acquiring this information about the Yew tree caused me to ponder why a few years previously I had planted a yew tree at my front door. What ancient memories had been stirred, causing me to do so?

The thorn trees in Glastonbury, England, are also considered sacred and are believed to come from shoots of the original holy thorn tree on Wearyall Hill. Legend tells that this first oriental-looking sacred Glastonbury thorn sprang from the staff that an exhausted Joseph of Arimathea thrust into the ground when he arrived on that land with his young nephew, Jesus.

Various symbols of the tree of life continue to exist in many countries and cultures. The Hindus revere the banyan tree for its longevity and powers of regeneration. Sacred shrines are often located at the base of particularly grand and far-extending banyan trees. Buddhists honor the Bodhi tree. Beneath its flowing branches is where the Buddha received enlightenment.

The tree is symbolic of our inner lives. It is one of the most frequent symbols that indicate the process of life, growth, unfolding, dying, and rebirth and also suggests these processes within our own lives. The folklore and symbolic narratives that associated these spiritual guides and teachers with the tree remind us that we too can ascend the tree of life to connect with and seek support from the spiritual worlds.

As you reflect on the tree drawing that you have just completed, ponder the size of the tree. Does your tree take up the whole page? If not, ponder the significance of being large, visible. What can a large tree offer that a small tree cannot?

Does your tree have roots? How deep are they? Is this tree, which is symbolic of you and your inner life, deeply grounded, or could this tree, be easily uprooted? Roots are said to be our foundation and show our connection to the Earth. They keep us grounded and nourished. A large tree needs large roots; otherwise, like a poorly rooted tree we can be easily toppled by the least gust of anguish blowing our way. Imagining we are a tree with large roots or doing similar grounding exercises such as drawing a deeply rooted tree can help us to remain firmly planted even when we are blown about by the turbulent winds of change.

My own experience of feeling disconnected from everyone and everything—even life itself—as well as knowing and feeling the positive effects that occurred in my life after I learned to reestablish balance and remain grounded, taught me to listen carefully for indications of this need in others. I acknowledge that grief and trauma affect not only our brains and their functioning, but also every aspect of our being, even uprooting our connection to the Earth.

Try this **grounding activity**. Imagine again, as in the guided imagery earlier in this chapter, that you are a giant tree. Extend your roots deep into the Earth. Experience your roots going down deep, deeper. Experience your roots going down, not only in a vertical direction; extend them as far as you can in all directions. When you have a good sense of your roots, open your eyes and note in your journal all that you sensed and experienced.

When we are not rooted in the Earth we feel ungrounded, separate and apart and can experience extreme anxiety and intense fears. When we reestablish our connection we again feel a sense of belonging and safety.

A number of years ago I created my first CD, *Journey to Healing*[7] because I recognized that most people I worked with, had lost their grounding. That guided imagery reestablishes the connection, not only to the Earth reconnects the listeners to their rightful place between Heaven and Earth. To reestablish that connection is to reconnect to the flow of Divine Energy and to all of the guidance and protection available through that sacred contact.

Ponder the activities that you have completed as a way to reestablish connections with your spiritual roots. What thoughts or impressions do you have as you ponder being rooted in the Earth?

The roots that appear in artwork, imagery and dreams can symbolize a variety of things and invite discussion on a number of subjects. Along with *grounding*, the words *source* and *history* are also often used in association with the word roots.

We all have experiences rooted deeply within; many of them draw us back to sources we know little of, sources that have in some cases been purposely blocked from us. Many Christians, for example, have little awareness that much of what they believe and practice flows from pagan roots—roots that were purposefully cut off and literally burned away in the numerous attempts by the church fathers to cleanse the "heretical memories" from the minds and hearts of the faithful. Few know that on the site where the Vatican now stands, there once stood a pagan temple. Here the ancients worshipped not Jesus, but another god-man whose miraculous virgin birth on December 25 was also witnessed by shepherds. Here, pagan congregations once glorified a redeemer who, like Jesus, was said to have ascended to heaven. On the same spot where the Pope celebrates the Catholic Mass in memory of Jesus, pagan priests once celebrated a symbolic meal of bread and wine in memory of their savior.[8]

Those influenced by Western thought have been indoctrinated to believe that Christianity and paganism are entirely antagonistic religious perspectives, yet the numerous resemblances between Christianity and the pagan mysteries are too numerous and too similar for any questioning mind and knowledge-seeking person to overlook. Even the teachings attributed to Jesus as "the only son of God" can almost all be retraced to earlier pagan sources, where they are attributed to other dying and rising god-men.[9, 10, 11, 12, 13, 14] In Egypt the god-man was Osiris; in Greece, Dionysus; in Asia Minor, Attis; in Syria, Adonis; in Italy, Bacchus; in Persia, Mithras. In Latin and South America, as well as in the southwestern United States, similar god-men have been a part of the traditional religions. There are stories of Kokopelli, who was born of a virgin impregnated by a God. This god-man taught the people how to remember their spiritual nature so that they could return to the stars.

After years of research, historians who have dared to ask questions outside the paradigm from within which they were raised have concluded that Christianity is not a new and unique revelation, but actually a Jewish adaptation of the ancient pagan mystery religions.[15, 16] Yet for 2000 years the West has been dominated by the notion that Christianity is of Divine origin, whereas paganism is the work of the Devil. The closer that one examines the data, the more that one is convinced the story of Jesus is not the biography of an historical Messiah, but a myth based on perennial pagan stories that were never meant to be regarded as historical documentation, but rather as metaphorical reminders of the god and human that each of us is. The Jesus stories and the teachings attributed to Jesus, like the pagan stories, the folklore, and the mythological stories told and retold around the world, are reminders of the forces of good and evil and that we must overcome the lesser aspects of our nature to know our identity, our own god-nature.

We have been indoctrinated to believe that pagan teachings and practices were built upon primitive superstitions. This is simply not true, for paganism was the spirituality that inspired the unequalled magnificence of the pyramids, the architecture of the Parthenon, and the philosophies of Socrates and Plato. These ancient philosophers were not simply academic as we know philosophers today; they were spiritual masters; they were sages, comparable to the Hindu gurus. They were mystics and miracle workers. Centuries later the miracles that these masters were reported to have performed were also attributed to Jesus. Like these Spiritual Masters of the Inner Mysteries, Jesus is said to have called upon the elements and applied their power to effect changes in this dimension.

Many traditional religions have adapted the ancient understandings associated with the healing and cleansing powers of the elements and have incorporated them into their doctrine and practices. There are many references to air, earth, fire, and water, as well as the uses of these elements, especially for rites of purification and blessing. The administration of the sacraments is a reenactment of traditional practices based on the ancient pagan understanding of the powers of the elements to connect us to what is Sacred and Divine.

Shamans and healers are connected to the Earth. Their Oneness with the Universe has been strongly maintained through traditional beliefs and practices. Even today they manifest powerful changes by drawing on the elemental forces.

Those from cultures less influenced by Western thought often have an easier time of reestablishing their connections to the Great Oneness than do those of us reared in cultures where our connections to the Divine Force in All and our connection to our ability to draw upon the powers of that Force have been seared from our hearts and brains. Yet, although it may take more effort for us to do so, the secret that sits in our centre still knows.[17] We each have a pagan heart and mind. We each have a pagan soul.

A few years ago it greatly surprised me when a colleague drew to my attention how immensely interested I had become in our energetic connections, the natural world, and its power to heal and cure. It was terrifying for her that I was sharing ways in which I was using energy work, tree imagery, and the elements for healing purposes. Stepping back from her reproach, I acknowledged that she had identified something that I now recognize as a natural progression in the course of deep healing. I have come to honor that the deeper each of us enters within ourselves, the more we come to know our own roots, our true self, our primal self, our soul self. Here the Elements, the Universe, and We are one. Here there is no separation. Here there is only Oneness. We recognize all of the forces of love that unite us. We recognize the forces of fear that keep us from knowing and experiencing this connection.

When we are able to stand in this Oneness, we too, like Jesus and the other god-men, can manifest miracles; we, too, can call on the Winds to be still; we, too, can put Earth on the eyes of the blind and marvel as they open; we, too, can call on the Rains to feed our corn; and we, too, can call on the powers of the Universe to heal us at a soul level, and we, too, can use this power to assist others as they find their way back to the Stars.

CHAPTER 9

# RE-ESTABLISHING SACRED CONNECTIONS

*I see in nature structure that must fill a thinking person with a feeling of humility.*

Albert Einstein

Early peoples associated their own spirituality with nature and naturally occurring events. Numerous stone carvings and other representations associated with their belief that the physical body of the Earth represented the body of a great and powerful Mother Goddess remain in various parts of the world even today. From the womb of the Mother Goddess all life emerged, and into her loving arms all life returned in death. The ancient Greeks named this goddess Gaia. At Delphi, the sacred conical rock called the Omphalos denotes the location of her sacred navel. A spiritual umbilical cord connecting Gaia and her children was attached to her navel, a link for her progeny in this physical world to the spiritual worlds.

We are again beginning to honor our Earth as an interconnected part of a great and wonderful creation as we come to more fully recognize that the Earth is indeed a part of a holographic universe and that, as such, her magnetic body, like ours, is energetic. The energy flowing through us from the Divine source moves through our bodies along a main energy pathway. Our major energy centers, our chakras, are located along this pathway. Energy also flows to every other part of our bodies along lesser pathways known as meridians. Similarly to the way that the sacred energy flows through our bodies along meridians, sacred energy courses through the Earth along energetic tracts known as Dragon Veins or Ley Lines. The belief that energy runs along pathways beneath the landscape is basic to the study of geomancy, which is central to many practices of divination, even to the practice of "witching" for water. The Chinese art of Feng Shui is also a form of geomancy. This practice is aimed at harmonizing human dwellings and activities with the associated Dragon Vein energy and therefore connecting the physical and spiritual worlds.

As in the human body, the pulse in the Earth surges more strongly in certain places. In the human body these sites are referred to as chakras and acupressure points. The flow of energy to the chakras, as well as to points along the meridians, known as acupuncture points, can be increased through healing practices. Knowledge of acupuncture points and an understanding of the direction of the energy flow associated with each meridian are fundamental to the practices of acupressure and acupuncture.

At places where the Earth's pulse is strongest and more easily perceived, our ancestors built enigmatic structures and conducted sacred ritual and ceremony. Singing and dancing, drumming, and flute playing were the means they used to stimulate and increase the flow of this energy along the Earth Mother's body in an effort to keep Her fully alive, thus ensuring their own physical and spiritual survival and growth.

Fertility rites and seasonal ceremonies were commonly celebrated at times of the year when the Earth's energy was most fully in line with the energy of the entire cosmos. The ancients used this knowledge to draw the powerful energy of the entire universe to the Earth and therefore to themselves. Many of the sacred sites located in the British Isles, Egypt, and numerous others parts of the world including the astrological sites near the ancient Mayan temples all demonstrate our ancestors' understanding of the relationships between the Earth's energy and the energy of the entire cosmos. Doorways and various other openings in many of the sacred sites I have visited open to the sun only during specific times of the year, times when our ancestors believed that the Earth's connections to the universal energies were strongest. Celebrations of the summer and winter solstices and the spring and autumn equinoxes were all manifestations of our ancestors' beliefs in the Great Goddess Mother and their understanding of the direct relationships between the natural world, the entire universe, the deity, and their need to maintain this connection to ensure blessings on their crops and thus their existence.

It is believed that many of the sacred sites worldwide, including the Neolithic sites in Europe, were constructed along these sacred energy lines. One such Ley Line in Southern England, known as St. Mary's line, connects Stonehenge, other Neolithic sites, and Salisbury Cathedral. Although it is dedicated to the Virgin Mary, it is believed the centre altar is built over a powerful ancient Goddess site.

The longest Ley Line in Britain, known as St. Michael's Line, links a series of chapels, churches, and cathedrals, almost all of which bear the name of the energy line upon which they are situated. These present-day Christian structures house statues that depict the Archangel Michael slaying a dragon. Building Christian structures over pre-Christian shrines demonstrates recognition of the relationship between these energy lines and the spirituality of the local peoples. Because the Dragon's energy, the energy associated with an Earth-based spirituality, was supposed to be fixed to the spot where the Dragon was killed, there is little doubt that the depiction of Archangel Michael's slaying of the dragon demonstrates the new religion's suppression of the Dragon's primordial power, and therefore the suppression of the spiritual strengths and beliefs of those who belonged to the Goddess traditions.

Many of the beliefs that our ancestors held were forced underground when they were overtaken by Christianity and they faded over time, but the belief remained strong that in certain places the human-divine connection can be more easily established. Such places continue to be referred to as *places of the in-between*. People from many cultures held beliefs that associated gods and spirits, fairies and gnomes with the in-between spaces in nature. They recognized that the Earth Mother offered places and spaces that afforded opportunities to connect with soul and spiritual forces. Openings to the underworld were often sites of sacred oracles. Through the crevices and hollows, through the cracks in the Earth's surface, our ancestors believed that they could more readily connect with sacred beings.

Earth people of today acknowledge, as did their ancestors, the sacredness of these spaces. Many are again recognizing at a deep level the need for their souls to once again be in relationship with the in-between spaces, places where contact with the spirit worlds can be made more easily, where human life and the spiritual worlds meld. There is a growing remembrance that not only is the Earth sacred, but also the forests, rivers, mountains, and other features of her living landscape are spiritual terrain—especially the places and spaces where one edge touches another.

Numerous authors and poets have penned the soulfulness of being in such places.[1,2,3] Many of our most sacred experiences occur during times and spaces that are in-between, spaces such as where the shore meets the ocean, where the grasslands meet the water's edge, where the mountains meet the sky, and where the prairie meets the forest. The in-between times occur at dawn and at dusk, at the change of Nature's seasons, as well as at the turning points that mark the changes of the seasons in our lives. The in-between times and spaces are sacred times, holy times. An energy surrounds these times that can be built upon and used as a catalyst to heal, for during these times we can be more readily tripped into a sacred experience, one that will help us to recognize that we do indeed have support and help from the spirit world and that we do indeed live, work, and play in parallel realities.

During my bleak mornings of grief and dark days of depression, days when I felt abandoned by everyone and everything, even by the universe, during the evenings of soul pain, when I lost all understanding of the God of my childhood and had not yet shaped the God of my now, and during the nights when I felt miserably alone and often somewhat suicidal, a teacher whispered: "Spend time alone gazing at the clouds, walking in the meadows, the forests, and by the water's edges. It will renew your spirit and rekindle your desire for life and to be among the living."

Those of us who acknowledge that the Earth is indeed sacred are beginning anew to honor this sacredness, to reestablish our connections to her and to redevelop our relationships with her landscape and with nature as a whole. In so doing, we are reawakening to the ancient knowing of the similarities to, and the connections between, the energy within the human body, the Earth, and the entire cosmos. Reawakening to this knowledge propels our use of these energetic connections for the purposes of healing and growth. Healers and therapists are daring to apply this knowledge as we not only create sacred ceremonies and redesign sacred rituals to honor the seasonal changes in nature, but also recognize and celebrate the seasonal changes in our own lives, in the lives of our loved ones, and in the lives of those we assist in professional ways.

Many who receive professional services from those of us who work in the helping fields have experienced significant emotional and spiritual pain; many have lived through traumatic events and now struggle with the numerous associated effects of multiple loss. Those who have not personally experienced such life-altering circumstances have little comprehension of the enormity of the impact of the effects of grief and trauma on human functioning. Few recognize that during such times every aspect of our humanness, including our interactions in relationships and our reactions to our work and other environments, are drastically altered. Many do not comprehend the many forms of trauma, nor the tremendous and over-whelming grief responses that we feel following a tragic life event. The effects of trauma can be experienced following wars, political torture, and terrorism; natural disasters; car, train, or plane crashes; domestic violence; child abuse; cult victimization; and assaults, murders, suicides, and other sudden deaths, especially child deaths. The most damaging mental, emo-tional, and spiritual distress results from trauma that is prolonged and repeated, trauma that entails an attitude of malevolent intent on the part of the perpetrator, and trauma that is deliberately inflicted—especially in a relationship in which the traumatized individual is dependent; at worst, in a parent-child relationship.[4,5,6]

Even though we might comprehend that traumatic events such as those just mentioned can leave one struggling with a sense of incompleteness, numerous other events and times in life that we and others do not fre-quently acknowledge can throw us off course and leave us struggling in a state of disequilibrium. We live in a world of change; with every change there is a need to let go of those aspects that keep us tied to the past. This can be a very pain-filled process. Changes can be developmental, such as sending our youngest child off to college, or situational, such as those that we face following a death, a job loss, relocation, a house fire, a burglary, or the robbing of a sense-of-self that almost always follows an act of sexual, physical, or emotional violence.

Some changes are chosen; others are imposed. Imposed changes rob us of control. The degree of control we have over any situation appears to influ-ence adjustment. It seems that when we are able to plan, to exert time and energy in anticipating the change and subsequent losses, we are better able to move through the experience. This is why the impact is profound when we face unanticipated death, deaths that are off-time, such as suicide or the death of a young person, or enforced change, such as being displaced from our country because of war, or sudden and unchosen job loss.

Every traumatic event causes changes in numerous aspects of life. For some, the changes may be enormous; for others, they may be less trau-matic. But all change carries with it aspects of loss. Losses are grieved, for what has been lost cannot be retrieved. For some, the changes may herald the loss of a past relationship and a planned future together. For others, the changes may include a need to let go of a longtime dream, a goal that can never be achieved.

Losses mean endings. Something must end before something can begin. We must let go of the old before we can take on the new. We resist change. Endings mean closures, saying goodbyes. The wounds left by what has been ripped from us can be very, very deep. Although the significance of a loss and the long-term effects are unique to each, the impact is felt in every aspect of our being.

Personal responses can be intense and lasting and can include living with pervasive fears, helplessness, and horror; existing in a world of desperation and brokenness; and feeling separate and apart from the mainstream of life and even from life itself. Traumatized individuals are frequently plagued by distressing flashbacks and nightmares; they may struggle with the powerful emotions that they experienced at the time of the trauma; and without treatment, many continue using the same self-protective means they initially learned (including the use of drugs and alcohol, aggression and violence) to buffer the pain and to shield themselves from the traumatic impact.

Those who have experienced significant grief and trauma are unable to focus attention for any length of time on anything other than the traumatic event and its effect on their lives. Long hours are spent trying to figure out what went wrong. Many experience immense forgetfulness and have difficulty making choices. The inability to think in clear and organized ways is often described as one of the most distressing symptoms of posttraumatic stress. Those who have been deeply wounded often doubt their own insights and inner wisdom; they dread anything unknown for they recognize the alterations in their thought processes. Many are wrought with feelings of helplessness, shame, despair, and hopelessness. Pessimism can dominate the belief system. The pervasive thought is that because misfortunes have happened, bad things will continue to be the norm.

Trust, faith, and hope erode. People who are deeply grieving, and those who have experienced trauma, are almost always in the midst of a spiritual crisis.[7,8] Beliefs are challenged and weighed against the lived experiences and often do not hold up under the scrutiny. The vacillation surrounding the struggle with beliefs and the attempts to find suitable answers to the numerous imponderable "Why?" questions can be excruciating.[9, 10, 11, 12, 13] That which was once not important becomes significant, and what was once of little significance is now paramount.

Over time, the physical body succumbs. Shoulders draw upward, almost to the ears. Aching backs and stiff necks demonstrate the need to release the overwhelming burden. This posture, characteristic of the physical responses to trauma, depicts a need to guard against further emotional and spiritual pain. It is also a clear indication that the person wearing this burden is breaking beneath its heavy robe. This robe, woven of numerous overwhelming feelings and emotions, including anger, resentment, guilt, shame, and regret, most likely contains the rough and worn fibers of a multitude of other unresolved issues and concerns. This heavy robe, although it is worn to protect against further hurt, paradoxically blocks the energy that is so desperately required for healing. Evidence of the decreased flow is testified to daily by those trained in holistic methods of energy transfer such as Reiki, reflexology, iridology, and acupuncture.

Numerous acupuncture points are located on the external ear. Meridians leading from these points carry energy to various parts of the body. When the shoulders are drawn up, as when the body assumes the characteristic posture of overwhelming grief and stress, the flow of Divine Energy along these meridians is markedly reduced.

At the beginning of grief and trauma healing workshops, I frequently have participants attempt a simple **exercise** that allows them to recognize how open or blocked to receiving Divine Energy they are. You might try this exercise as a self-assessment of your openness to receiving energy from your Source.

To begin, turn your head to the right. Pay attention to how far you are able to turn it. Pay attention to how stiff, how sore your neck is as you do so. Now return your head to its normal position so that it is once again in line with the centre of your body. Keeping your nose directly in line with your navel, take your right hand and move from the top of your right ear to its tip, pinching the ear five or six times. Starting again at the tip of your right ear, repeat the pinching activity; repeat this step five or six times, each time moving from the top of the ear to its tip. In doing this action, you are stimulating a large number of acupressure points, which in turn increases the flow of energy through the meridians of your body. After you have completed the pinching, turn your head again toward the right side of your body. Pay attention to how stiff, how sore your neck now feels. Did the stimulating of the acupressure points make a difference? Was it easier to turn your neck after you stimulated the ear's acupressure points?

Now turn your head to the left and notice how stiff your neck is on this side. Using your left hand, stimulate in the same way the acupressure points on your left ear lobe, and then test the effects on that side of your neck. If you experienced stiffness and soreness when you turned your neck either or both ways, I recommend this exercise as a part of your healing routine. Do it each day until the flow of energy moves more adequately through your body of its own accord.

My own experiences of brokenness and my long journey to healing caused me to travel many roads to investigate and apply ancient and alternate forms of helping. As a therapeutic helper working in the areas of grief and trauma, I now listen for words of brokenness and for indications that perhaps those I work with require helping and healing strategies that are currently outside the realm of Western health care practices. I now recognize that somehow the shock that we experience upon hearing tragic news breaks our energetic connections, interfering with our ability to draw universal energy to us and through us, leaving us feeling out of sync, out of or off balance, and very disconnected.

During my own time of extreme brokenness I experienced many of the signs and characteristics associated with being out of sync and off balance because of the decreased flow of energy to and through my body. I found the experience of cognitive dissonance most difficult to cope with.

Although the term cognitive dissonance has various meanings, I use it to refer to the experience of feeling that somehow we have become separated from our own thoughts. I initially recognized this syndrome as I attempted to contribute during health care discussions. Although I had once been excellent at decision making, during my days of brokenness I dreaded engagements where I would encounter this challenge. I could mentally conjure up solutions to the issues at hand that, based on my education and professional experience, were likely effective alternatives, but when I attempted to communicate these ideas, I was unable to articulate my thoughts. The garble that poured forth made little sense to my own ears, and the bemused looks from committee members informed me that they too had heard my utterances as confusion.

A healer described my communication difficulties as an indication that my brain had been "split" by the trauma, thus affecting the ability of the life-force energy to cross from one side of my brain to the other. This affected not only my ability to communicate my ideas, but also my ability to walk in balance. The healer asked me to simultaneously raise my left arm and left foot. This I did with little difficulty. She next invited me to simultaneously raise one leg and the opposite arm. Her response to my need to stabilize my stance was that I was "out of synch" with the rhythm of the Earth.

At that time I did not comprehend her assessment or diagnosis, but I now use her activity when I am assisting others who have experienced trauma. I recognize their need to again be in sync with the heartbeat of the Earth Mother to relieve the out-of-sync and disconnected feeling they are experiencing. You might like to do the following **exercise** as a self-assessment.

From a standing position, simultaneously raise your limbs on the same side of your body, and then repeat the activity using opposite limbs. Note your physical responses to this exercise. If it was difficult to maintain equilibrium when you were attempting to balance on one leg while holding the opposite arm in the air, it would be valuable to ponder your own need to reestablish energetic balance.

To reestablish energetic balance, I was encouraged to connect with "rock people." Rocks are a huge portion of the natural world, but they are generally considered inanimate and lifeless. Yet for centuries healers used rock medicine. Because of their connecting and electromagnetic properties, rocks are today used to draw both physical and emotional pain from the body and to draw spiritual energy to those who use their medicine. This element is considered to have such powerful connecting and healing properties that the rock is often lovingly and respectfully referred to as a Grandfather and given the place of Wisdom in the North on the Great Medicine Wheels of the world.

Following the healer's teachings associated with the use of rock medicine, each morning for the next 12, I did an exercise to reconnect the flow of energy between the parts of my brain and my body. Standing, facing the rising sun, I began. With legs spread and hands held high above my head, holding in each hand an ocean-washed rock the size of a closed fist, I first drew in gold-colored energy light from Grandfather Sun with the intention that this energy would penetrate and heal the masculine aspects of my being. Guiding the golden light energy into the rock held in my left hand, I sensed the light move down my arm, across my neck, down the opposite side of my body, out the sole of my foot, and into the earth below.

After experiencing the golden light energy move through my body, I made an intention to balance the feminine aspects of my being and proceeded to draw silver-colored energy from Grandmother Moon into the rock in my right hand. As before, I sensed the light enter the rock in my right hand, flow down my right arm, cross over at the nape of my neck, flow down the left side of my body, through the sole of my left foot, and enter the earth two stories below. The results were incredible. While I continued the exercises for the full 12 mornings as prescribed, the positive effects of this healing on my abilities to articulate in clear and concise ways were rapid and astounding, both immediate and long-term.

A right brained experience such as this always forces me to go to the library to validate in a left brain logical way what has occurred; and so it was in this instance. The many hours of searching proved fruitful in numerous and various ways. I was fascinated to learn of the significance of the number 12. I had pondered the need for 12 rock-medicine treatments. I discovered that in numerology, 12 represents the union of the sun (1) and the moon (2) and that the union of the sun and the moon represent the joining of our higher and lower self, a connecting within us of the energy from above (the Heavens) and below (the Earth).

I also found scientific evidence to help make cognitive sense of the spiritual teachings and guidance that the healer had given me, much of it to do with the effects of trauma on brain-hemisphere functioning. Our brain is divided into two hemispheres, a left and a right. Each hemisphere has its own way of knowing, its own way of perceiving reality. In a manner of speaking, each of us has two minds, two consciousnesses, mediated and integrated by the connecting cable of nerve fibers between the hemispheres.

The left hemisphere is associated with cognitive and analytical functioning, reason and logic, and the development and use of language skills. The right hemisphere is more closely associated with intuition and things of the heart. The right hemisphere is the hemisphere more linked to things of a spiritual nature than to those of the cognitive mind. The right hemisphere is associated with the unconscious, with creative thought and creative activities, imagery, and dreams.

In normal functioning the hemispheres cooperate, with each half contributing its special abilities. When we wish to communicate a creative idea, for example, an automatic transfer takes place from the right hemisphere to the language centre located in the left hemisphere. What we are thinking is what we are able to clearly articulate. It is believed that this automatic transference of information from one hemisphere to another is a developmental process strengthened by the movements children make as they learn to crawl.

Since 911, the study and pursuit of best practices for treatment of post-traumatic stress disorder have focused on the effects of trauma on the human brain. The findings have helped to explain, at least in part, the mental and emotional symptoms following trauma, including the experience of being unable to articulate what one is thinking and feeling.

The amygdala and hippocampus are parts of the limbic system within the midbrain which process incoming sensory stimuli on their way to the cerebral cortex. These two structures have major functions in processing life events and their sequencing within the life narrative. The amygdala processes and facilitates the storage of emotions and reactions to emotions. The hippocampus processes and stores the data so that they make sense in terms of context related to time, space, and sequencing of events (When did that happen? What happened next?).

During the normal course of life, together the amygdala and hippocampus process and store both the event and the emotions attached to the event. During trauma this often does not happen; the emotions are stored (amygdala), but often without the context of the event (hippocampus). This is because the amygdala appears to be unaffected by stress hormones whereas increasing stress levels appear to suppress hippocampus functioning.

Since the hippocampus requires the use of language for both processing incoming information and recalling that information and since it is suppressed during trauma there is a growing awareness that trauma healing must happen in ways other rather than solely through the use of language. This has been increasingly recognized with the advent of magnetic resonance imaging to measure brain activity. Lanius and her colleagures[14] confirmed that persons who experience a traumatic event and are suffering from posttraumatic stress replay their traumatic memories through the sensory and imaging storage area of the brain's right hemisphere.

Currently, there is great interest in the information-processing functions of the right and left cerebral hemispheres and their relationship to the limbic system. The right hemisphere appears to play a greater role in the storage of sensory input. The amygdala appears to be the limbic structure through which sensory information travels on its way to the right hemisphere.[15] The left cerebral hemisphere is much more closely associated with the functions of the hippocampus.[16]

The way that the limbic system responds during trauma means that distressing emotions, confusing behaviors, and impulses can all exist (amygdala) without access to the information (hippocampus) that created them. Without healing, traumatic memories (amygdala) never integrate into the life narrative (hippocampus). They remain as though frozen in time, separate from the owner of the experience. Yet "healing trauma requires a linking of all aspects of a traumatic event."[17] Linking the traumatic events to the rest of the life narrative, requires making and remaking links between the brain's left and right hemispheres.

Because speech and language are viewed as highly developed functions, the left hemisphere has for many decades been considered the dominant hemisphere. The scientific approach with its methods of deduction was developed to engage primarily the left hemisphere. Educational systems, including those that offer training to helping professionals, were developed from this approach. Techniques designed to suit these models focus almost solely on the use of language. Yet the evidence now suggests that traumatic memories are more closely associated with the right hemisphere than the left, and during trauma Broca's area in the left hemisphere, which is generally responsible for speech production, is often suppressed.

Traumatized people need information, for it gives their cognitive mind the answers that they seek regarding the effects of trauma. Excellent counseling strategies and the use of therapeutic language skills are essential, but in and of themselves, left hemisphere strategies will not heal trauma. Left hemisphere language skills are used to help people cope; they appeal to the cognitive mind and to the mental aspects of trauma. Trauma affects all aspects of humanness. To heal trauma, strategies must be holistic in nature. To heal trauma, we must focus on where the trauma is stored and processed; therefore, we must also address the needs of the right hemisphere.

The right hemisphere is more closely associated with things of the heart and the soul. Its language is symbol and its voice is creativity. For generations, following a traumatic life event, healers used experiences that engaged more fully the brain's right hemisphere than the left, including music, drumming, dance, and the symbols that appeared in the person's dreams and art. They used ceremony and sacred rituals. They drew on the healing powers of the elements—water, wind, rock, fire—and in the many forms of nature.

Their intention was to heal the soul pain and call back the spirit energy that had left at the time of trauma. In using soulful strategies, they were addressing the needs of the brain's right hemisphere. In speaking the language of the soul, they were going to the very seat of the stored trauma.

For some years I have been keenly aware that soul concerns are the issues that most frequently fester beneath the surface of any unhealed trauma and that this pain is rarely addressed in traditional trauma therapy. Because the right hemisphere is more closely associated with concerns of the soul than with those of the cognitive mind, and because my main focus in any therapeutic endeavor is the healing of soul concerns, it has become imperative for me to increasingly incorporate right hemisphere engaging strategies into the trauma healing work that I do. Because as human beings we require both hemispheres to function as an integrated whole, and because I have so frequently heard "My head and my heart no longer work together," it has become essential also to incorporate techniques into my trauma work that help to reintegrate the two hemispheres.

I truly believe that Spirit was encouraging and guiding the soul healing process I was to incorporate, for it was not long after I started sharing my ideas and introducing others to these techniques that I was offered a contract to offer weeklong healing sessions to a group of people who had experienced significant trauma. It was obviously an opportunity to test my theories and combine my professional education and years of clinical experience based on Western medicine with the knowledge and skills I gleaned from numerous other systems of health and healing, as well as the positive results from the application of these methods to my own life.

With the intent that the focus for the first day would be on the integration of the energies between the two hemispheres, I brought small journals, one for each participant. As we explored the topic, I invited each to describe what he or she already knew about the concepts being presented. This strategy, which I previously used with other groups as an empowering technique, now took on an additional purpose—a method of engaging participants' left hemispheres. After each member contributed to the groups' learning, I paraphrased their thoughts and added a small amount of new information. Although this technique was also my usual way for braiding old knowledge with new, I now did it not solely as a teaching strategy, but also as a way to further stimulate their left hemispheres, their cognitive minds.

Concentrating then on my desire to cross over the information, I immediately moved the participants into an experiential activity, this time not only to reinforce learning, but also to stimulate their right hemispheres. As they worked, tranquil background music played to additionally stimulate the right hemisphere and thus the soulfulness of the experience.

As the participants began to complete the experiential portion of their learning, I encouraged them to reflect for a few moments on what they had created, on the colors that they had used, and on any symbols or metaphors for their own lives that had appeared. I asked them to ponder the impact of their final product. After this time of reflection, I invited them to capture in their journals their impressions and insights. I not only asked them to document what they experienced, but also encouraged them to note what they saw—what they believed their creations revealed. I reminded them of the power of art forms, guided imagery, and other creative activities to reveal soul messages and encouraged them to trust what they believed was being mirrored to them.

Reflecting on the soulful experiences, such as a guided imagery or creative activity, and then capturing the experience in written form gave the participants a further opportunity to transfer thoughts and information between the two hemispheres. Reflection is a right brain activity; writing requires engagement of the left hemisphere. I felt certain that by reflecting on their experiences and then journaling about them, the participants would engage in a brain hemisphere crossover activity.

I had had many previous positive experiences, both personal and professional, with using the process of externalizing. Externalizing an experience helps to capture and retain the images and feelings associated with that experience. When a soulful right hemisphere image is captured in written form, the cognitive mind receives the food it requires for sense-making and for storage of the images and the experience in memory. It will be there, waiting to be reexamined and perhaps worked with in more detail, in the future. For these reasons dream therapists encourage the practice of journaling as soon as possible after a dream.

Following the completion of their journal entries, I invited the group members to share any portions of their experiences that seemed significant while the remainder of the group listened respectfully and intently. Although group processing was not new in the work I did previously, this time, as I engaged the participants, I did so with an additional purpose. This time I encouraged the sharing as a further way to externalize—to make sense of their soulful experiences.

Because the language centre for most people is located in the left hemisphere, giving words to a soulful experience helps the cognitive mind make sense of the experience. Verbalizing the perceptions of the right hemisphere helps to ground these perceptions in reality. This is why, when we describe the scenes and events of a dream, we begin to comprehend the meanings behind the symbols.

Witnessing the energy shifts in the participants as well as in the group itself, as the participants moved from the knowledge portion to the experiential portion of the day's content, was truly miraculous. Witnessing the shift as they moved from the right brain experiential activity back to engaging the left brain through the use of written and oral language was awesome. Hearing the effectiveness, hearing words such as healing and transforming, was inspiring and encouraging. I knew that the application of this four-part process made as significant a difference in the healing and lives of these group members as it previously made in my own.

Convinced that this four-part process effectively provided information and encouraged healing, I began to apply this methodology consciously and consistently. Because of such positive outcomes, this process became the methodology for my practice and teaching efforts.

## The Four-Part Process for Healing Trauma

1. Appeal to the left hemisphere by braiding new *information* into that which is already familiar.
2. Offer an *experiential activity* to supplement the new information, including a guided imagery or a creative art activity to immediately engage the brain's right hemisphere.

3. Provide the opportunity for **reflection and journal writing**, a process of continual movement between the right and left hemispheres, a crossover process that encourages healing and balance as it moves the information and "energy" across hemispheres.

4. Encourage **processing** the experience to fully engage both the right and left hemispheres. Express the ideas and images captured in a soulful experience, and receive empowering feedback from the facilitator and group members. This process appears to reinforce the crossover, greatly helping to make real for the cognitive mind the soulful experiences that have taken place.

I have now used the *Four-Part Process for Healing Trauma*[18] with more than 4,000 people of various ages, of both genders, and from a variety of cultures. The positive effectiveness of this methodology in opening doorways for entry to soul-level work is phenomenal. Although others apply a number of these steps, I strongly encourage consistent use of the Four-Part Process, for I cannot overemphasize the deep and lasting healing that takes place when these steps are followed in a conscious and consistent manner.

Through the course of my professional life I have done considerable work with individuals and groups. I now know that although in the past I was doing good work at the physical, mental, and emotional levels and even touching the souls of others, I was not doing soul healing. Not until I provided an opportunity for people to experience their own creativity and reflect on the messages mirrored from their own souls did this depth of healing happen.

Although it is said that people are predominantly right or left hemisphere dominant and that, culturally, we are predominantly one or the other, I believe that this is more a process of nurture than an unchangeable fact. For the most part, in times past, knowing was gained through personal experience. It is only in recent decades and especially in the cultures of the West that the goals of teaching and therapy have been to gain the attention of the left hemisphere in an effort to impart the knowledge and beliefs of others.

Until the beliefs of others are tested they remain a belief. Experience moves the belief to a level of personal knowing, and personal knowing is an important aspect of soul healing.

Each time I engage people in a healing experience, each time I shift the focus from a cognitive level to a soul level, from a left hemisphere to a right hemisphere experience, I witness an amazing shift in the energy and countenance of the individual as well as of the group. Each time I hear people sharing their experiences, I listen for acknowledgement of their shift to a new level of personal knowing—for their recognition of having shifted into the space of the in-between, into the space of the sacred territory of soul. I now recognize that as we shift from trying to make sense of the world in a cognitive way to viewing it in a more intuitive way, that as we shift from our left hemisphere to our right, we enter one of those in-between spaces. It is in those in-between spaces that things of significance, mystery, magic, and sacredness happen.

Although I have now witnessed this shift many, many times, each time I am in awe; each time I am aware of the privilege. I know I am walking beside another as he or she enters more fully the place where true healing—soul healing—happens.

# CHAPTER 10

# CREATING SACRED SPACE

*There are more things in heaven and earth, Horatio,*
*than are dreamt of in your philosophy.*

William Shakespeare, *Hamlet*

Early one morning I received a call from a woman I had assisted years pre-viously as she moved through a difficult grief experience. As often happens when one transcends such pain, Barbara made significant changes in her personal life. She returned to school and was now a graduate nurse working in community palliative care. Her frantic voice that morning indicated an urgent need. Although I anticipated tragic news, I was unprepared for the desperation she conveyed upon her arrival. Anxiety and fear punctuated each word and every action. Her entire countenance and affect were visibly altered; an undistinguishable heaviness cloaked her. Through uncontrollable sobs, Barbara relayed that at seven in the morning of the previous day she had entered the inner-city apartment of a man diagnosed with end-stage cancer, intending to administer scheduled pain-relieving medication. Her bed-bound client had requested that the door to his apartment remain un-locked so that his friends might visit at liberty. Upon arrival at her client's home that morning, Barbara noticed a large woman on the floor, slumped over an overstuffed furry toy. Barbara's resuscitation attempts, as well as those of the paramedics she had summoned for help, were unsuccessful.

As Barbara related the incident, my initial thought was that, being new in her position, she likely felt guilty over her lack of success in saving the woman's life. Barbara quickly revealed that this was not the case and went on to tell me that she did not feel at all herself. Each time she closed her eyes, "the face of that woman is right there. I can even see her looking out of my very own eyes." A chill coursed through my being as she uttered those words, for I knew instinctively knew what had taken place. Sensing that it was necessary to use every skill I had ever learned, I began a breathing technique to help shift consciousness. In that moment of intense focus, and for a brief second only, I viewed Barbara at another level—at a soul level. What I witnessed made me gasp, for I was now seeing not only around, but also throughout Barbara, the same heavy energy I had sensed when she first entered my office. This grey heaviness completely engulfed her, making it impossible to distinguish her individual presence from that of a much older and larger woman. In earnest desperation, I begged, "O GOD, HELP ME WITH THIS ONE!"

Although the prayer makes me smile as I write it, I can still hear myself uttering those pleading words, for I knew what was being required of me, but I was very aware that I really did not know how to do it. Yes, I had removed spiritual intrusions under the guidance of a shaman-teacher, but my shaman-teacher was nowhere near. Nor did I believe that Barbara was someone who would be receptive to a lengthy Shamanic ritual and somehow time seemed to be of the essence.

Following the guidance that I felt I was receiving in answer to my call for help, I led us both into a deep meditation. I asked for gold light to enter our crown chakras and guided the golden light through our entire bodies, grounding it through the soles of our feet and into the Earth. I called to the dead woman's guides and angels. I asked them to be with her. I spoke to the dead woman and informed her that she had died and that she did not belong in the body she had inhabited. I told her that it was safe for her to go to the light, that guides and angels were present, and that they wanted to and were ready to take her to the light.

In a split second an enormous stream of brilliant light entered Barbara. Engulfed by two large, very strong beings of radiance, the dead woman's energetic presence was lifted and swiftly propelled upward to the right and outward through my office walls.

Barbara jolted as the energy shifted. Immediately, the persona I knew to be hers was once again present. I had no need to inform her of what had taken place; she saw and experienced the circumstance as I had. I encouraged a Reiki-energy treatment to complete the process and seal the protective layer of her aura. I believed the shock of seeing the dead woman in her client's room had broken the protective layer of her energetic field, thereby allowing entry of the disembodied spirit.

In the years when I practiced strictly from within the medical model, when I viewed humans as physical beings who happened to have souls rather than as spiritual beings who happened to have bodies, I would have been completely unhelpful to Barbara and to the spirit of the woman who had entrapped herself within Barbara's form. I believe that I was given this experience to teach me what I needed to know next. I am aware that, had these events occurred years previously, Barbara might have continued to be in "psychiatric" distress, and the woman's spirit might still be earthbound. As it was, Barbara was able to leave my office within the hour, and, although I invited her to return for follow-up, she telephoned the following day to inform me that she returned to work and was feeling "just fine— bewildered, but just fine!"

One more time and in one more way the boundaries of my worldview expanded, and I was permitted to view one more form of soul entrapment. One more time I was asked to recognize that when we work with the spiritual aspects of human life, the spiritual forces of the light assist when we call for their help. I asked for their help and received their help in assisting another into soulful freedom. In turn, I learned a great lesson.

In The *Unquiet Dead*[1] Edith Fiore suggested that the use of brain-toxic products such as cognition-altering drugs, intoxication, loss of consciousness, and shock-like experiences create opportunities for the entry of disembodied spirits. This happens because these circumstances can damage the human aura. When the protective layer of the aura is not intact, a disembodied entity, entities, or other forms of misplaced energy, some negative or even harmful, can invade and inhabit. When there is energetic interference, behaviors can alter significantly. A person whose energy field is inhabited by an outside influence can experience alterations in every aspect of his or her being. The inhabited person may take on personality characteristics of the invading entity, even manifesting behaviors diagnostic of psychiatric symptoms.

Damage to the protective layer of the human energy field can also happen as a consequence of trauma and abuse, especially during sexual trauma and when the abuse has been repetitive. The damage tends to be the most extensive when trauma happens early in life. A child's aura is delicate and fragile and not yet well fused to his or her physical body.

Many I worked with have personally lived through as well as witnessed horrendous and repeated acts of physical, mental, emotional, spiritual, and sexual violence. As a result, their psychic space, their sacred space, was damaged. Frequent and violent invasion of the protective layer of the human energy field can result in numerous tears or fractures of various sizes. Because of the tremendous amount of aura damage, those who have experienced trauma are often open targets for all types of misplaced energies.

Misplaced energies lodged within our psychic space are sometimes referred to as spiritual intrusions, which can be in the form of disembodied spirits, as in Barbara's case. When people die, if there is great fear about their next existence (based upon teachings that they received about the outcomes of their lives), instead of heading for the light that opens as the body dies, the spirit may hide from it. Recognizing the need for a physical body, the spirit may seek someone whose fractured aura allows easy entry and then hitchhike.

Many who experience the intrusion of a disembodied spirit intuitively recognize their circumstance. They tell of the voices that seem to have invaded them, yet do not belong to them. Others share their awareness of times when they knew they had picked up the "vibes" or when, following a specific event, they began to recognize that they were behaving in foreign, frightening, or uncharacteristic ways. For some, freedom from this invasion, this entrapment, is their primary reason for seeking help.

Misplaced energy from sources other than those of disembodied spirits can also become lodged in a damaged, underprotected aura. Because our aura is a manifestation of our holographic nature, we are a part of the All, and the All is a part of us. Because of this we are impacted by the energies that surround us, energies of both a positive and less-than-positive nature.

An intact aura acts as a shield. When we are well protected, we are more in charge of the energies that penetrate our aura; a strong shield acts as a filtering system, allowing in only energies of high vibrations. When our aura is damaged, we are not well protected. When our auras are damaged or weak, we are open to all the energies in our environment, even those of low vibration—energies that may be much less than positive, or even harmful to us.

Whether or not you have previous knowledge of these concepts, you have probably been, at least at some level, aware of this information. You know, for example, that you enjoy being close to some people, whereas you feel "prickles" when others come near. You are also aware that some people make you feel good while you are in their presence. They seem to radiate peace and calm and are able to make an entire room and everyone in it also feel that way; others can quickly turn any situation into chaos. Examine this in energetic terms. Can you identify what is happening, energetically, in these situations?

During a recent workshop on providing trauma care, I taught professionals the above notions to help them recognize their need to shield and protect from the misplaced energies that surround their work. Following the initial session, a therapist addressed me with the comment:

> "Isn't all this information about energy and the energetic perspective on trauma simply opening us up to negative energy?" "Well," I responded, "energy, in both its positive and less-than-positive aspects, is real, and you are already open to both these influences. The important information is to know how to fill yourself with the positive aspects and send that forth from you and how to protect yourself from the less-than-positive effects of your work. It is, I believe, also important to know how to help those we work with to connect to the positive sources of energy and to shield and protect their energy fields from the less-than-positive influences that impact them.

I then involved the group in the following **art activity**. You might like to complete it as well, for this art activity will assist in advancing your comprehension of the notion that as holographic beings, we are the sum total of all the energies that move into and out of our energy fields.

Gather some chalk pastels of various colors and a large sheet of paper to complete this activity. A flipchart-size sheet of newsprint works well. Visually, divide the page in half, and on the left half draw a gingerbread-body shape, similar to the one you drew in a previous chapter. This shape will depict your physicality. Using a different color for each, add all of the layers that represent the various aspects of your holistic nature. Now, on the other half of the page, draw a second gingerbread shape. Add all of the layers of the aura to this figure as well. As you do so, note how the layers of the first figure overlap the aura layers of the second. Gently stroke each pastel color of the first figure, moving the colors into the aura colors of the second figure. Then stroke and blend the colors of the second figure and move them into the colors of the first figure. Note your observations and insights. Are you able to more clearly recognize how, as holographic beings, our thoughts, emotions, feelings, attitudes, words, actions, and therefore overall spirituality affect every aspect of other human beings?

Do we ever really have to tell another we like or dislike him or her? At an energetic level, this information is picked up long before we have the cognitive abilities to put this knowing into words. Can you recognize why it is important to send only positive thoughts and words to those we work with, to our partners, to our children, and to the world in general, rather than to project dismay, dissatisfaction, fear, and worry? Are you able to see how those around us readily pick up our vibes and how our vibes can affect every aspect of their being?

Most of us do not acknowledge how much we actually are a part of the holographic universe and how influential we are because of that. We must each become more cognizant of how we constantly affect and are affected by the energies surrounding us. We must each become more aware of how the energies of others on this dimension and the energies from other aspects of the universe, all aspects of which we are a part, affect us each and every moment of our lives. We are affected to a greater or lesser degree, depending on our abilities to shield and protect our energy fields. We must each know how to cleanse our aura of misplaced energies, and we must learn how to build a strong, protective shield to block all unwanted and harmful energies.

Although for some years now I have been helping people to cleanse and seal their auras, I was first introduced to this work during my study of the use of energy-transfer-healing modalities. During the initial course a classmate explained that the aura can sustain damage and therefore need mending. I was skeptical of the notion, but her ideas were quickly rein- forced. Upon arriving home that evening, I discovered in my mailbox Edith Fiore's book *The Unquiet Dead*,[2] left there by a friend who asked for my review. The similarity between Fiore's message and my classmate's caused me to ponder such possibilities, and the knowing was quickly revealed.

Within weeks I accepted my first contract to work with traumatized women. In those days I was only very occasionally seeing auras. On the first day of that group work, as one woman briefly shared an experience of child- hood trauma, I saw her aura flash around her. To my amazement, not only did two areas lack color, but the dark areas also appeared to be missing something, as though something had been ripped away.

The image impacted me deeply and lingered for weeks. Although I felt that I was being asked to make a difference, I had absolutely no idea how to assist. I had nearly given up hope that my prayers for assistance would be answered because up to the second last day of the course I still had no clue how to mend a fractured aura. The night before this group was to complete its 10week session, I received the knowledge I needed not only to help this woman but also to help many others in similar situations.

In a dream I experienced a huge red willow hoop descend upon and completely surround me. The hoop was similar to a dream catcher, the webbing encasing me from top to bottom, side to side, and front to back. Using sinew attached to brightly colored beads, a Native grandmother was mending a tear in the webbing. As this image faded, a flowered wreath descended, once again completely incasing me in all directions. This time a purple ribbon wove itself in and out of the wreath, clearly defining its edges, making its colors radiant and vivid. As gently as this image had appeared, it faded, and one more time I was encased in a large hoop. This time the hoop was made of gossamer fabric. The fabric surrounded me completely, about one arm's length in all directions. This time, an angelic-like being arrived carrying a large needle. I had the sense that the needle was made of solid gold. It was connected to shimmering thread being unraveled from a gigantic spool, also made of gold, which was part of an enormous spinning wheel. Using the gold needle and thread, the angelic being reattached the fabric in two places where it had become disconnected from the hoop.

In times past, when a person experienced a circumstance such as trauma or a loss of consciousness, a shaman or healer would quickly assist in the cleansing and resealing of the aura. Because most of us in our modern world do not have access to a shaman, and trauma robs us of personal power, it is valuable for each of us to do what we can to regain our sense of self and thereby ultimately reclaim our power.

The following guided visualization supports this philosophy. It places you in a circumstance where you can work with your own spiritual forces to make important and necessary changes. It offers you an opportunity to recognize that, when they are called upon, the spiritual helpers assist, and that, in and of itself, is empowering. During this visualization you will be guided to cleanse your aura, the sacred space surrounding you.

To call upon and receive spiritual assistance with the cleansing of our own sacred space heightens immensely our abilities to take back what has been stripped from us. This is an enormous step toward reclaiming personal power, an enormous step along the road to healing.

To begin, close your eyes, place your feet firmly on the floor, and consciously connect with your breathing. Pay close attention as you allow your breathing to become steady and even... in and out... in and out... in and out. Give yourself full permission to be completely absorbed in this moment in time. Just trust that for right here and right now you are safe and protected, and that this is a very safe, very easy, and very effective exercise.

Now gently inhale deeply. Imagine that you can move the breath up to the crown of your head. Raise that breath, way, way up, as though you were sending it high into the universe. Now sense a beautiful gift of light being given to you in exchange for your breath. Imagine this wonderful gift of beautiful light in whatever color or colors seem right for you. Sense this very bright light beginning to flow down to you.

Experience the light entering the crown of your head; allow the light to move gently into your head. Sense or feel it filling your entire face. Allow the light to enter your neck and move into your chest. Experience it flooding and filling your entire chest. Feel the light moving downward, completely filling your abdomen. Allow the light to move into your pelvis; give it permission to fill your entire pelvis. Move it over your thighs. Move the light into your knees, your lower legs, your ankles. Move the light into your feet; sense your feet filling with light. Feel how full and heavy your feet have become. Experience some of the light seeping from your toes. Sense the rest of the light beginning to move out the soles of your feet; allow light to flow steadily from the soles of your feet. Imagine it moving deeply into the heart of the Earth. Notice that, as the light moves from you, it carries with it all that is no longer working for you. Continue to be aware of the heaviness in your feet. Recognize how firmly planted your feet are on the floor.

Now, one more time, inhale deeply. As before, move your breath up to the crown of your head; raise your breath way, way up, as though you were sending it high into the universe. Now sense a beautiful gift of light being given to you in exchange for your breath. Imagine this wonderful gift of beautiful light in whatever color or colors seem right for you. Experience the light beginning to flow down to you. Allow the light to enter the crown of your head. This time guide the light right to the centre of your chest, right to your heart chakra. Focus on the heart chakra, and begin to experience the light expanding, getting bigger and bigger and brighter and brighter. Allow the light in your heart center to seep from your heart into your entire body. When you experience your entire body glowing with light, push the light from you with the intention of filling your entire aura with glowing light. Keep pushing the light until you have completely filled the space around you.

*Now, using your inner vision, gaze at the sacred space surrounding you. Look all around. Is there any energy there that does not belong to you? If so, call to your spiritual helpers of the light, your guides, angels, spiritual grandmothers. Sense a radiant being standing right beside you, waiting to assist. Witness this being of light bringing a sacred cleaning tool into your aura. Using the cleaning tool, the being of light begins to move all around your aura picking up all the energy that does not belong to you. Sense the being of light moving all around, all around, all around, and all around your entire aura as the cleaning tool picks up all the energy that does not belong in your sacred space. Experience it moving around, and around, and all around your aura as many times as necessary until all the energies that do not belong to you are cleansed or tightly contained within the cleaning tool.*

*When all the energy left in your sacred space is of the light and belongs to you, sense the cleaning tool being withdrawn. Witness the cleaning tool, which now contains all of the foreign or dark energies moving far, far, far above you. Pay close attention to the magic unfolding. Recognize the transformation. See the cleaning tool and all the energy it contains disintegrate. Sense it change into bubbles of the most magnificent colors. Experience the energy change into sparkling, glittering bubbles of light. Notice the bubbles catching the breeze. Sense them floating on the breeze, high, high up, and far, far away. Know this transformed energy can now only be used for good.*

*Breathe a prayer of gratitude, and gently and easily allow yourself to come back fully into the present moment. Take in a huge breath, and become aware of how much lighter you feel.*

When you feel ready, reflect on any images that may have appeared, and then journal your experience as completely as possible. I encourage you to gather some art supplies and externalize in any art form of your choice the most significant aspect of your healing experience. Alternately, you may want to complete an **art activity** that reuses the six-foot aura image you previously created. To do so, gather colored papers of various textures, including tissue papers and shiny foil to represent the brightness surrounding you now that you have cleaned your aura—shined your halo, so to speak! Crush small pieces of the colored tissue and foil, dip them into white glue, and place them on your aura image. Doing this van Gogh–like technique gives a three-dimensional effect, adding the sense of the splendor that we often experience and witness when we examine our cleansed auras with our inner vision.

I recently guided the above visualization during a workshop session for counselors, helping them to strengthen and maintain strong boundaries and thus prevent vicarious trauma. Following the visualization and reflection time, I invited the participants to use whatever art medium they wanted to externalize their experience. A young man was amazed at what had taken place. He shared his feather-decorated artwork and reported that the three ancestors who had come to help him had cleansed his aura by using an eagle's wing. He stated that they jokingly told him they needed to be present so that he would "get it right." They encouraged him to breathe into areas of his aura that he immediately recognized as his "vulnerable places," as his "weak spots."

On another occasion, following the above visualization, a participant made a collage of a gigantic, silver and white, glimmering angel pulling a large Shop Vac. The woman reported her satisfaction upon witnessing the Shop Vac for she felt that only a strong, durable cleaning tool such as this would be capable of clearing away the years of darkness that she believed engulfed her.

After these empowering inner journeys and the opportunity to process their experiences, this man and woman were ready to proceed to the next step of their healing process; mending the tears in the protective layers of their auras. If you believe you are also ready to do so, you can use the guided visualization on my CD *Shielded with Light: A Guide for Cleansing and Sealing Your Aura*.[3]

With an intact aura we automatically feel stronger, for we are then not continually being drained of, or leaking, precious energy. After our aura is cleansed and sealed, we must then begin to build and continually reinforce a strong shield of protective light around us, for the stronger our shield, the more protected we are from being penetrated by misplaced energy. The more spiritually protected we are the more at peace we feel.

Each morning I visualize a brilliant shield of colored light surround me. When I sense that the light is one arms length above me, one arm's length below me, behind, in front and to either side of me, I affirm: "From this shield of love and light only good things can come from me and only good things can come to me. I am safe. I am divinely protected." I teach each person I work with to cleanse and seal their aura and then to visualize a protective shield of love and light. I invite you to do the same.

# CHAPTER 11

# RECLAIMING LOST WHOLENESS

*One of the greatest privileges of a human life*
*is to become midwife to the birth of the soul of another.*

Plato, *The Symposium*

In our world today there is profound disillusion with organized religion and scientific materialism. The root cause of this disillusionment seems to be a deep desire to restore lost wholeness, to heal the gaping wounds in our individual souls and within the collective soul of humankind.

A philosophical underpinning of the past ages that has aided the loss of our individual and collective wholeness is the notion that the human soul is beyond wounding and brokenness. Those in positions of helping, who hold this as fact, have limited, if any, ability to hear experiences of soul pain or to acknowledge the reality of soul fragmentation, much less to offer strategies to reintegrate the fractured human spirit individually or collectively. Yet for our tribal ancestors and for Indigenous peoples around the world today, notions of soul wounding and brokenness and the intrusion into the human spirit by an unwanted or evil entity is very real. Shamans and healers respond to the brokenness by retrieving the lost soul parts and to the spiritual intrusions by removing the unwanted entities.

Deep within each of us is a distant familiarity and appreciation of this ancient knowledge. Although in ever-increasing numbers modern-day shamans are reclaiming the skills to offer soul healing, the majority of therapeutic helpers still have not found ways to put their innate knowledge into professional practice. A major cause of their lack of follow-though seems to be a need for more extensive understanding of the interrelatedness and interconnectedness of the physical, mental, emotional, social, and spiritual aspects of human beings.

Recently, while I facilitated a psychoeducational program, *Journey to Hope and Healing: Beyond Trauma and Abuse*,[1] a young woman, Yvette, told me that for years, regardless of the circumstances, the combined smells of alcohol and stale cigarette smoke caused her to flee to the bathroom, where she would vomit violently. Although Yvette had some sense of the origin of this physical response, she was unable to determine why she would often smell alcohol and stale cigarette smoke, even in their absence, and have a need to vomit as a response to the smells. During a therapeutic session Yvette made the connections between the smells and the traumatic experiences she endured during childhood. From an early age, until she ran away from home in her teen years, Yvette was sexually violated by her father. The sexual abuse generally happened during the early hours of the morning, following a night when her father had been drinking heavily. The combined smells of alcohol and stale cigarette smoke and the way her father smelled during his incestuous attacks became associated in her mind with the sexual abuse. Her flight into the bathroom to vomit after each of those early experiences also became associated with a way to discharge the effects of the experience and regain some sense of control over her father and his forced attacks. Whereas during early childhood, vomiting resulted from her need to rid her system of her father's semen, in later years vomiting happened as a reaction to her associations with how he smelled. The vomiting often occurred even in the absence of abuse.

During the abuse her cells stored the memories of how and where her body was touched and how that touch felt. Her cells stored memories of the sights, sounds, and smells surrounding the events, as well as the emotional responses to them. Emotional responses of fear, terror, anger, rage, shame, guilt, and powerlessness infiltrated every cell of her being. Her cells also stored memory of the methods she used to regain some sense of balance and control, as well as her emotional responses to these methods. In future years her response of vomiting became associated with the smells alone, even in the absence of physical contact. The vomiting became associated with the best way to gain some sense of personal power over a situation in which she felt powerless.

In reviewing recent vomiting events (in the absence of alcohol and cigarette smoke), Yvette quickly recognized that in each situation she felt controlled and powerless to change the outcome. Relying on previously stored information, her physical body responded in the best way it knew how. In the past, vomiting had been a way to regain a sense of control. Her cells knew that this response had released some of the stored emotion, and her body continued to respond in the same manner in future situations when similar emotions were aroused.

Our physical bodies are an accumulation of the energy generated around each of our experiences. Emotionally charged thought forms created as a response to each event are stored in cellular memory. The energetic vibration attached to any event is a direct outcome of our perception of the event. Stored memory of the emotional charge that resulted from past events influences future events. The greater the intensity of the emotion attached to any past event, the greater the degree to which that event influences future events.

Stored memories affect our lives in numerous ways. As in Yvette's case, daily events can trigger stored emotions. The trigger can be a sight, a sound, a smell, a memory, a photograph, the life story of another, someone's behavior or actions toward us or others, such as a touch or a hug. Words, tone of voice, the way that another holds his or her body, or even the way that he or she looks at us can awaken past memories. The behaviors of another may be innocent and well intended, yet they may trigger within us highly charged emotional responses, including fear and resentment, anger and mistrust. The trigger causes us to flash back to a previous time. Disrespectful behaviors and language can stimulate memories of past terror, especially in circumstances in which the trauma was intentionally inflicted.

It is important to recognize that the trigger is not in the word, the smell, the sight, or a story told by another. The trigger is in the association. The trigger is in the meaning that was attached to the sight, smell, objects. We generally use the word *trigger* in reference to the emotional responses that result from stirring memory stored during a difficult life experience, but we also respond to the stimulation of positive memories in much the same way. We respond to triggered memories, both positive and terrifying, in almost identical ways as we did when the memory was first formed.

When they are triggered, the emotions stored at the time of the initial event are reactivated. Although the event was in the past and the emotions being stimulated are from the past, we re-experience the event and the attached emotions in the present moment with the same intensity as at the time the event took place.

Many who have experienced trauma—especially repetitive traumas and most especially when the traumatizing events occurred early in childhood— have learned to emotionally disengage and psychically detach from the circumstance by dissociating themselves from the experience. To dissociate from an experience is to literally "go away" to a place where the emotional, mental, and spiritual anguish and the physical pain of the experience cannot be felt. When I asked, "Where did you go?" one woman who had frequently been abused in childhood responded, "Far, far, far, away." Another stated, "When I knew I could not get away, I left my body.... I was off standing by the door watching. My body was there; it was like a shell." Many relate their experiences of dissociating within a spiritual context: "The angels always lift me away"; "I was held in the arms of a beautiful woman in blue; the Virgin Mary, I think"; and "Jesus always came. He would tell me I would be okay."

Although dissociating from a physically or emotionally painful experience may at first appear to be a positive strategy, especially when it involves connection with a spiritual presence and associated feelings of spiritual protection, it is important to recognize that dissociation can also have less than positive side effects. Because we first learn this strategy during a time of terror, any time that we are triggered to the point where we flash back to an experience that initially caused us to dissociate, we will likely repeat this coping strategy as a way to once again escape the emotional and physical impact. Because some, especially those who have experienced extensive and repetitive trauma, use this coping strategy so effectively and so frequently, they can find themselves spending a lot of time disconnected from reality, and as much, or more, time out of their bodies, as in them.

During a recent meditation class I witnessed the form of a woman, the exact likeness of the one who was positioned directly across from me, move from her body. I spoke to her spirit-form, and after providing assurance that the experience was safe, invited her spirit-form to return to its physical home. I knew this woman well, so during the break I informed her of what I had witnessed. She was not surprised. For many years she had fled her body when she was abused. She indicated that being asked to "lie down and relax" when she was feeling anxiety, triggered memories of her uncle's comments during incestuous experiences, experiences that her spirit had become adept at escaping. Because of her adeptness at leaving when triggered, the process of dissociation was interfering with the effectiveness of the healing approaches she was using. During dissociation, the mind, the eyes and ears, and parts of the soul are absent. Following the discussion of my observations, she stated it well: "For me, making the choice to heal means making the choice to stay."

A further detrimental effect of dissociation is that when we leave, aspects of ourselves may not return. Whereas dissociation and personality fragmentation are relatively new psychological terms, these notions are ages old. As noted earlier, these ideas have since ages past been recognized in Shamanic cultures.

According to Shamanic beliefs, circumstances that shock the body can shatter the soul. During a soul-shattering experience, a part or parts of the soul and its associated characteristics may flee in an effort to escape an unbearable life situation. In Shamanic cultures a shaman performed rituals and engaged in practices such as soul retrieval, with the intent of bringing back the lost soul part to its human dwelling. In such cultures these practices were basic to the care given to a traumatized person, for it was believed that when soul parts and their associated characteristics are missing, the person is incomplete and therefore unable to function to the fullest of his or her ability.

Dissociation can result in personality fragmentation, and the fragments sometimes have their own names, psychological functions, and sequestered memories.[2] Many therapists, trained in today's mainstream methods of helping, do not yet identify the numerous ways in which emotional and physical trauma can impact the soul. They therefore do not comprehend that, to be truly helpful, they must also assess, as did our Shamanic ancestors, for soul wounding and then be able to apply strategies that will mend the fractured human spirit.

In *Journey to the Sacred: Mending a Fractured Soul*, I described my own experiences with soul fragmentation.[3] I told of how in September of 1985 the traumatic pain of losing a child shattered my soul. Like Persephone,[4] I was picking flowers in a beautiful garden one day and lost in the darkness of the underworld the next. Life had been bright and glorious, but on that mid-September morn, all disappeared. I had fallen through a trap door and was being held a prisoner in the *oubliette*. Held in the darkness, I was abandoned and forgotten.

For 10 long years I wandered dispiritedly, searching in the shadows for a way out, searching in the darkness for what had been lost. Yes, I was searching for my lost son, but, more accurately, I was searching for my lost self, for the parts of me that had gone away, and for the characteristics that had gone with those parts. I knew I could not lift the shroud-cloud until I found the objects of my search.

My desperate need to reclaim the lost aspects of myself led me to study ancient Shamanic methods of helping and healing. During those sage-filled days of summer I connected with the animal spirits that came to assist me as I studied, as I healed, and as I retrieved the soul parts that had been in hiding for such a long time.

Because of my own experiences of healing and reclaiming my wholeness, I now recognize and acknowledge the Shamanic teachings and practices regarding soul loss and soul retrieval. I work with people who are grieving the many losses in life. I hear their stories of soul's emptying and of their need to reclaim the lost aspects of themselves. I have learned to listen for phrases that indicate when someone has experienced soul loss. I frequently hear statements such as "I feel so empty," "I feel broken," "I feel lost," "I feel so incomplete," "I am not whole," "I am always searching," "I don't even know what I am looking for." Those who use these expressions can also often share dreams in which they find themselves searching for something that is missing. The most telling dream symbol associated with a need to reclaim a soul part is that of searching through a house.

You might like to take a moment right now and draw a house. When you have completed the **art activity**, study it carefully. Does your house have a door, an entryway for your soul? Does your house have windows? Can soul see beyond the four walls? Do you have windows on all stories? Sometimes we have the ability to see what is on the lower levels, yet not the ability to see things of a higher nature. Does your house look lived in, with curtains on the windows, smoke coming out the chimney, or does it look vacant, abandoned?

A house is the most common dream symbol that indicates consciousness—the home of the soul, the place it dwells during incarnation. When soul parts are missing, the recurring dream of searching from empty room to empty room is common. As healing happens and as soul parts return, the dreamer will often have further dreams in which the rooms are beautifully decorated and now filled with light. When the house dreams cease, a person is generally able to communicate a sense of now feeling much more whole. There is an innate awareness and a great sense of satisfaction in knowing that all the soul parts are home.

Although I was guided to Shamanic practices to understand soul loss and as a way to seek help with the retrieval of my own soul parts, I have since learned that this work has been done in various ways in various cultures. Sometimes, as well, a soul part will return voluntarily. This tends to happen when a person is earnestly engaged in doing his or her healing work. A major task in getting a soul part to return is to convince the part that it is now safe. In many ways this is accomplished by reestablishing the trust that automatically occurs during the process of extensive self-care and healing.

Soul parts can also be retrieved in an almost voluntary way during other spiritual and healing practices. In my first book[5] I described assisting a young woman in her early 30 in retrieving a soul part that fragmented upon hearing the traumatic news of her brother's death. In that situation the soul part, a filament likeness of her 30-year-old self, slid into her heart chakra as I transferred energy during an energy-transfer healing treatment.

In the therapeutic work and teaching that I now do, the strategy that I most frequently use to retrieve a soul part or parts is deep-trance work. While people are in trance, I guide them on an inward journey, a journey to the core of their being. The great advantage of using this method of soul retrieval is that rather than having someone else in charge of their healing, the person does their own soul retrieval. Having been successful with the process, he or she can more readily own the results. This in turn helps in the reclaiming of personal power —the power stripped away as a result of the traumatic event.

Because many who are attempting to heal from trauma have a lifelong history of abuse and terror that often begins in early childhood, I like to begin the work of healing by reacquainting the person with the younger aspects of his or her soul self. It is important to note that it generally takes a fairly difficult event to produce soul loss in an adult. This is not true for children. A child's aura is easily fractured, and once fractured is more open to the potential for a soul part to escape. Second, because the hippocampus, which is a part of the brain's limbic system responsible for recording content and context (who, what, where, when, how, why), is not fully functioning in early childhood and because even a fully functioning hippocampus can shut down during a stressful experience, a traumatized child has little capacity to respond to a situation in a logical way. The amygdala, also a part of the brain's limbic system, functions before birth and is on "peak alert" during trauma. Its job is to record and store emotional content. So when a child experiences trauma, he or she stores the emotions surrounding the event, often without the contextual information. Even years later a lot of emotion can surface when such an event is triggered, and this can happen with little contextual memory to substantiate the feelings.

When I guide someone on an inner journey to find and reclaim a fragmented soul part, I simply say, "Go to a time early in life, when it hurt so badly or you got so scared, that a part of you went away because it just was not safe to be here any more." In response to this nudge, the person will usually immediately return to the very place where a difficult incident occurred. When located, the soul part looks identical to how the person looked at the age they were when this particular soul part fragmented. Too fearful to return, the soul part remained in that very place, as though frozen in time. Recently, a woman who was afraid of the dark found the likeness of her two-year-old self, still locked in the tool shed. Moments later she discovered a three-year-old likeness beneath the water, a part of herself that had remained at the scene of a family boating incident.

Many First Nation Canadians, who were placed in a residential school during early life, feel the need to return to the school in a soulful way and reclaim the soul parts that were left behind. One man found his little one still crying in the principal's office and then found another part of him alone in a dark cloakroom. One 70-year-old woman retrieved a frightened six-year-old from the same bathroom where she had been raped by a janitor on the first day of her residential school experience.

During the *Taking Flight Trauma Recovery Certification*[6] program, I teach a process for safe and effective soul retrieval work. Since there can be moments of intense emotional pain when contact is made with a soul part that has remained in the original place of trauma, it is important that soul retrieval work be facilitated by a care-provider who has been trained and is skilled both in working with those who have been traumatized and in the use of soul healing methods.

Part of doing such work is to learn to do it with great integrity. A therapeutic helper must always be cautious of, and conscious of, the level of readiness of the persons they are assisting. It is important to understand that although some are physically, emotionally, and spiritually ready to move into the place of surrender, others are still very reluctant to go to those deep places. It is understandable that we want to bring everyone along on the same path of clearing, but we must move through the past only with those who are ready for such clarity. In doing healing work we must always develop an understanding of the willingness and comfort level of those we are walking beside. When we do so, we offer an incredible service that brings healing to all aspects of humanness, one that empowers, beyond measure, both the giver and the recipient.

A second important part of doing soul retrieval work is to know that soul retrieval is a multi-step process, and that each step is of equal importance. It is vital to know each step well, for only then can a facilitator be alert to any need to adjust a particular step, so as to ascertain that the healing will be complete and the benefits sustained. The steps in the process are: relocating the hidden aspects of the self, making each part feel a sense of safety, welcoming each of the parts home, celebrating their returns and then reintegrating each of the returning soul parts into the greater self.

When a part of the self, a soul part, is located, the person is encouraged to say and do all that is required in order to make that particular part feel safe, and to then update this part to the present reality. This can take some time because a soul part that fragmented during a time of intense fear will have remained in the original place of terror and will have little, if any, idea of what has taken place since that time.

I encourage those who are doing their soul retrieval to inform each newly located soul part about all the other healing work they have done, and how much they want the part to return, so that they can be whole and complete. I invite the person I am guiding to tell the soul part that they are now in charge of their own circumstances and will do all in their power to ensure that when this part returns to them, it will be kept safe. This inner dialogue is all necessary to convince the soul parts, especially those parts that are still terrorized, that they are welcome and can now safely return.

After each of the returning soul parts are welcomed home, the process of integration begins.

The effects of soul retrieval cannot be missed. Most people know immediately that something incredible has happened. They state how differently they feel, even though some are unable to identify what exactly the differences are.

Over the years I have witnessed the return of soul parts on hundreds of occasions. The peaceful glow that surrounds people during the welcome-home ceremony never ceases to fill my own soul with radiance and joy. It is as Plato noted: "One of the greatest privileges of a human life is to become midwife to the birth of the soul of another."[7]

Following the welcoming home ceremony, I encourage those who have received this form of healing to sit in silence for a few moments and to then, if possible, go for a walk, preferably in nature. On the walk, they are to notice sights they have not noticed before, to listen for sounds they have not heard before. They are encouraged to pay attention, as a child would, to the details, to pay attention to the increased brilliance in the colors and the increased clarity of the sounds in nature.

Upon return from their time in nature, I discuss celebration. I encourage that they celebrate the experience fully, as a way to acknowledge the return of their soul parts and as a way to honor this major step on their journey to wholeness. Some choose to do a nature activity; others choose an activity such as decorating a balloon or a cupcake for each returning part. Whatever celebration activity is chosen, it is important that it is done wholeheartedly. Along life's journey we must each learn to celebrate our healing progress and to celebrate it fully! We must each learn to celebrate more than we mourn, and when a soul part or parts have returned there is something incredible to celebrate.

Next in the process is a discussion of the reintegration journey. I remind those who have just experienced a soul retrieval healing of the promises they made to the returning soul parts. I encourage at least three days of self-nurturing behaviors to make sure that the initial reintegration remains solid and then remind the person that the reintegration process can take several months, since each of the returning soul parts will also be bringing back its associated soul gift or gifts. When I teach this notion, I like to draw the outline of a large gold circle, and within that circle I draw many small circles. On each small circle I write a word that describes a soul gift, virtue, or characteristic, including joy, beauty, creativity, trust, hope, love, peace, laughter, truth, playfulness, and honesty. I explain that when a soul part leaves, along with it goes a particular soul gift or characteristic. People who have been deeply wounded easily relate to this visual image. They know that they have lost these characteristics and often use phrases such as "I no longer feel joy," "I have lost my creative spark," or "I never laugh any more." Feeling the loss and emptiness, yet not knowing how to get back what they lost, many attempt to fill the void and numb the pain with drugs, alcohol, sex, food, or other addictions. Soul retrieval is not a panacea, but I believe that it is basic to trauma work. When the broken-away parts are reintegrated, there is no longer the craving to fill the empty spaces. Once the soul parts are reintegrated, the traumatized person is much more successful in all the other healing work that he or she attempts. It is difficult, if not impossible, to face and work through those concerns from a place of intense soul brokenness. With an intact soul/self, people are more capable of accessing all their soul gifts and characteristics, all of which are necessary to move their lives forward.

Over the first few days and months following soul retrieval the person will likely experience a return of the characteristics that fled when the soul part left. I invite them to pay attention, and to welcome the characteristics home. I encourage the person to notice the age of the returning parts and not to be dismayed if for a time some responses and reactions are more similar to the responses of a child that age, than of the adult self. Each returning soul part needs time to integrate fully back into the soul's larger essence, and the larger soul self must learn what it is like to once again have that aspect as an aware and responding part of the whole self.

It is important to enjoy those immature experiences and view them as delightful, for the soul parts are expressing their characteristics, and these are always positive. Soul characteristics include joy, happiness, laughter, creativity, love, peace, beauty, courage, harmony, trust, hope, and gentleness. Perhaps in expressing their characteristics in ways we would consider to be immature, the returning soul parts are teaching a joyful process of learning some new ways to once again be as soulful as a child.

Occasionally, a person is unsuccessful in the first attempt at soul retrieval. This is often related to a need to first complete some other healing work, as well as to issues surrounding trust. The major developmental task for a young child is the establishment of trust and when trauma happens in early life, the very development of trust is hampered. Because the soul part must feel very sure that things have really changed, and that it is now safe to return, the initial process may need repeating a couple of times. When this happens it is usually valuable to wait a month or so between efforts, thus allowing time for the integration of other healing work.

Recently, during a healing workshop, I led a guided journey to help participants retrieve soul parts. Tears flowed as participants recognized aspects of themselves that they had previously been unable to connect with. Following self-nurturing with hugs and lullabies, they invited the little ones into their heart centers so that integration could happen. One young man shared the joy and resolution he had experienced. He stressed that he had been "working so hard to heal," and he "needed a sign." He longed to know that he was "making some headway in [his] healing efforts." He emphasized that years previously he had caught a glimpse of his "little inner boy." The child was "dirty and frightened." "He hid behind something and would not come to me…. But today, the minute he saw me on the path, he came running and jumped right into my arms." The integration was complete. The young man could once again know the characteristics that had remained inaccessible to him since early childhood. Having reclaimed this younger part, this man was ready to take a further step on his journey to wholeness.

If you know that soul retrieval is an important next step for you I encourage that you find a therapist who is certified in trauma recovery and skilled in doing soul retrieval work. You might choose to purchase my CD *Reintegrating Parts of the Self*.[8] When you do so, take the CD with you to your therapist so he or she can guide you in how to use my work to supplement the healing work you are doing.

---

# CHAPTER 12

# BRINGING PEACEFUL CLOSURE

Mother's quilt provides a warmth,
Beyond its fiber down.
Each night I'm wrapped in love,
Our family history and my wedding gown.
Mother cut with care her patterns
Each scrap to trim and save—
Just as she did with the numerous fabric remnants
that to her, others gave.
Each patterned square reveals a story
Of our family's growth and change.
It is far better than an album, for this memento speaks to me
Of many precious moments the camera did not see.
Part of each marriage ceremony was mother's quilt-gift to the bride.
It makes me smile just to recall the sparkles in their eyes.
Lambs and teddy bears announced each baby's birth,
And pink and green pajama scraps retell of Christmas mirth.
When winter days were turning cold and all the canning done,
Daddy would set the frame up firm, for quilting time had begun.
I'm so glad I still can hear them today, as I am wrapped
Inside this priceless heirloom that warms me as I nap.
There you are, Mom, I see you... among the colors bright,
In your kitchen dresses, gingham aprons, and your gowns for night.
They all remind of you and of the things that you've been through,

The smiles and tears, the strife, but mostly of your teaching of the wrong
   and of the right.
My quilt would not have been the same without your understanding care,
My sorrow and joy are sewn in, and hemmed by time and prayer.
Our lives were joined by chance they say; I believe by choice—and this is
   my great pleasure,
For a quilter of love and story like you is indeed a priceless treasure.
It matters not that my coverlet is frayed and has tiny little tears;
Years of life and warmth and time have helped to put them there.
So I wrap myself inside your quilt and feel your love and care,
And dream of how I will impart to those I leave behind,
The strength and courage you have shared with so many of humankind.[1]

In preparation for our mother's 90th birthday, my sister requested that each of mother's children photograph the quilts Mother had over the years given to us, our children, and our grandchildren. My sister was designing a "quilt book." Clipping and snipping, she was fashioning a chapter for each of Mother's children. Our individual stories were being braided into the story of Mother's life, symbolically depicting her sharing of each of our journeys as we moved through the hills and valleys of our own experiences.

Although Mother did not live to view the final product, the overall goal for designing the quilt book had been achieved. For it was the process, the very undertaking of its creation, that achieved the outcome. The process unlocked memories and stimulated the telling and retelling of stories—of narratives that needed to be shared and reexamined to ease past hurt and thereby weld generational bonds.

Even though she had not been ill when the idea for the quilt book was formulated, I recognized that for about two years previously, my mother had been actively engaged in conducting her life review. I initially observed little notes inside some of her teacups and tags attached to other treasures that indentified the person to whom she desired the object to be bequeathed.

I was also aware that during this period Mother spoke much of her relationship with her own mother. I had never before heard her speak of the things she discussed. Most significantly during these conversations, she dared to say things that had been less than positive about her childhood and her early life. My mother lived the motto, "If you can't say anything nice, don't say anything at all." Yet this unaccustomed behavior, her descriptions of events the way that she saw them, and the sharing of her emotions around these circumstances were an important part of the sorting and then of the reframing of the aspects of her life that had not been the way she would have liked them to be.

A number of decades ago Eric Erickson[2] and Robin Butler[3] described the process of life review. Erickson viewed life review as a time of "determining if the gods are pleased with the life that has been led." Butler perceived the life review to be a time of doing a "balance sheet." According to these developmental theorists, in doing a life review we examine the life we have led and conclude with feelings of integrity—that we have done the best we could—or with feelings of despair—that our life has not turned out the way we would have liked. Therein, is a great opportunity for those of us who walk beside others in their times of processing the events and circumstances of their lives.

My father's final life review was quite different from my mother's. In creating her quilts, she was able to leave behind some very tangible evidence of the mark she had made on the lives of those she influenced. The dialogues that flowed about the creation of that legacy aided her life review and allowed her to experience deep feelings of satisfaction and integrity. My father, according to today's standards, died young. He lived only a short time following a terminal diagnosis and was never able to return home to order the arrangements of his tangible effects.

Over the years I have recalled his life review. I am now aware that an important part of bringing closure for him meant being able to bless the various aspects of his life. I believe that he desired to know that he had done the best he could. As I review my journey with him, I also believe he longed for reconciliation with those circumstances in which he felt he had not done the best that he could.

My last visit with my father began three days before his passing. I had known him as a man of few words, so the intensity and depth of the conversation we shared about the life we had spent together marked me indelibly. My father stressed that he wished he "had been able to do more for [me]," "to give [me] more." My simple response, "Daddy, you gave me life; you gave me my education. I could ask for nothing more," affirmed the roles that he had played in my life. His balance sheet, in which he had placed me on one end of the teeter totter and him on the other, was now in balance. Little more needed saying. My father was able to rest, knowing that he could now bless the aspects of life that he had shared with me. I, in turn, was able to bless the aspects of life that I had shared with him.

Although the life review is initiated by a life crisis, including the crisis of receiving a terminal diagnosis, it is also engaged in as a part of completing the normal developmental tasks of aging. I have noted that, regardless of the circumstances that initiate the process, the pace seems related to the urgency as well as the length of time required to bring a satisfactory closure to the life and relationships that are ending.

Reminiscence, an important aspect of the life review, can be activated by visits, photographs, history books, news reels, music, song, art, etc. These things naturally stir memories, but each can also be used in a therapeutic way.

For a time I was a nursing director in a long term care facility. I like to sing, and I often sang for the residents. Their selection of songs would almost always bring a number of the residents to tears. Because I was intentionally using song as a therapeutic way to stimulate memories, I would later spend time with each teary-eyed resident, exploring the memories that had surfaced as I sang. They relived and re-enjoyed happy memories and found ways to release the emotional load attached to the difficult ones. In many cases, all that was required to release the difficult memories was to share their painful stories.

The therapeutic goal in assisting others during their life review is to gently guide the process in a direction of increased self-worth and to help them to see their lives as a meaningful whole. Even though some may initially view their life as bleak, every life is made up of positive and less-than-positive circumstances. Any therapeutic work in this regard must focus on assisting the other in recognizing that every event has many possible outcomes. People often need to be reminded that when we move through a difficult life experience, the difficulty tends to saturate consciousness; and most of us, at one time or another, require assistance with viewing the positive aspects that have resulted from what initially appeared to be a very difficult circumstance.

I was often reminded of this when I worked with women in the prison system. They frequently emphasized that had they not been sentenced, they would likely no longer be alive. These women had reframed their circumstances. They had identified some constructive outcomes from what had initially seemed very bleak experiences. The self-evaluation in which they engaged was similar to the process that Butler referred to when he recommended doing a balance sheet as a way to evaluate life.

When I assist with a balance-sheet exercise, I ask the person to list, in chronological chart form, the major events in his or her life. If the one I am working with is unable to write, I create the chart as he or she lists the events. I treat this work with the highest regard and the greatest respect, trying continually to remind myself of the need to completely accept this person and his or her life circumstances and view of reality. I believe that assisting with a life review is sacred work that allows me to peek into the soul of another.

Many times the balance sheet work is all that is required to move people through any emotional turmoil that has surfaced as they review their life. In listing the major events, most are able to acknowledge that although there were difficult times, their life was also made up of numerous grand experiences. Others, however, require more direction. In such cases I find it valuable to ask that person to identify any positive long-range outcomes that arose as a result of the difficulties. Circular questioning such as "Tell me what happened after that," followed by "And then what happened?" and again followed by "And then what happened?" are often valuable in helping distressed people to recognize the positive outcomes that flowed from an initially difficult event.

Creating a balance sheet helps most people to release the emotional load of their life's hurts, but it is also essential to acknowledge that some have had incredibly difficult life circumstances. When it seems impossible to find the positive outcomes from life's painful experiences, I sometimes find it valuable to rely on the collective contributions of the generation with which the person most strongly identifies. The strongest generational identification usually occurs between 20 and 40 years of age. Questions that can affirm the contributions of the cohort group for persons who are in their eighth or ninth decade might be "How did your family manage to survive the depression?" or "How did your troop win against such odds?" Affirming others and acknowledging their strengths tells them that we recognize that, based upon their life's circumstances, they have done the best they could.

We tend to view our past happenings out of context, which is not therapeutic. We often judge the past based on the knowledge, education, strength, skills, and resources that we now have. If we were to place ourselves in the exact circumstances that we are now judging, most likely we would make a similar choice. It is valuable to recognize this and to acknowledge that the desire to change things from our past suggests forward movement along life's journey. It means that we have grown and, because of that, can see things differently. And when we see things differently, we will desire to do things differently. It is important to affirm that, "Yes, I would make different choices now, but back then I did the very best I could" and "If I have a chance, I will make different choices next time." Such affirmations, although a necessary part of assisting another, are also of immense personal value when they become a part of our own inner dialogue.

We tend to think of life review as a process that happens prior to death, but it actually takes place throughout our lives. Although dying people do a major life review in an effort to bring satisfactory closure to their lives, we each do a life review every time we move through a significant life change. We do a life review any time that we must adjust to a circumstance after which life, as we knew it, will never again be the same. Such circumstances include the loss of a body part, a career change, relocation, or the loss of a loved one (to death, separation, or divorce). We do a mini life review each time that we come to a turning point, and each time we must examine what we have accomplished or become.

Turning points are times of spiritual renewal. The turning point itself can be a time of intense turmoil, and it is often the catalyst that drives us inward. The process of life review is stimulated by soul. It is a call from deep within to examine what needs to be changed, what needs to be cleared, what needs to be balanced. It is a process of setting our internal affairs in order. It is a process of releasing the bonds that hold us in fetters, prior to our next great movement forward.

A turning point is often accompanied by intense and dramatic dreams. Dreams that surface during such times are those that we have no difficulty recalling. A year prior to my mother's death I had two dreams that foretold this turning point.

My mother was in her 89$^{th}$ year, strong and healthy. She was fully alive and vibrant. She lived alone and drove her car to visit and minister to people in the hospital and nursing homes of her small village. There was no earthly reason to believe that she would die within the year. Yet as I pondered the dream messages, I knew that I was being given an opportunity to complete any unfinished business that might remain between the two of us.

She spent her last months in a palliative care suite in a long term care facility, and I spent many hours at her bedside. This time together was a privilege and a gift. It afforded an immense opportunity for spiritual growth and for the advancement of my knowledge of the spirit world. I took full advantage. Although my mother was conscious and orientated to all three spheres (time, place, and person) to the end of her life, she spent many hours in a trance-like, rapid eye movement state, a state of wakeful dreaming. After wakening from one such dream I said, "Mom, are you dreaming?" She nodded. "I am having the most incredible dreams." I asked her to tell me of them.

In the beginning her dreams seemed life review–like. She related dreaming of things and events in her life that she was trying to work through and resolve. Sharing these dreams gave her an opportunity to examine these events in an objective way. The information she was receiving from her dreams helped her to examine what she needed to review and heal so that she could leave this life with her teeter-totter in balance. As she related the dreams I was able to help her to recognize that some of the dreams were encouraging her to see some events in new ways.

As her illness progressed, the dreams provided a bigger view, an overview as it were, of her life. In one of these dreams she saw herself as a young woman dressed in a beautiful red dress. My dad came to pick her up to take her dancing. The plan was that they were to be driven to the dance. The car never arrived, but my mother kept her red dress on anyway and danced and danced and danced all around the farm.

My parents were married at the start of the depression. My mom was young and beautiful, as symbolized by the beautiful red dress (the color of life and vitality). There was much promise, I am sure, of a life that would be full of music and dancing, but somehow it never happened. Life on the farm was hard, but my mother never stopped hearing the music. She danced and danced and danced all around the farm, for many years of marriage. Her dream was, I believe, affirming a job well done.

During her final days the dreams seemed to be more connected to the future that she was seeing than to the life she had lived. She related that her brother Joey, who had died a number of years previously, had come to take her for a ride in an airplane. She expressed immense joy and happiness as she described the fun that they had: "He took me really high, and we went really fast. He did somersaults, and we laughed so hard. He took me all over. He showed me the most wonderful sights. But then I had to press the red button. He told me it was not my time yet and that I had to come back." My mother was being guided gently in and out of her body. When the final time came, she would know the route.

The shift in my mother's dream life paralleled a shift in her interests. I was cognizant that she no longer desired to discuss the past or to hear about the day-to-day events of her family or community. The spiritual aspects of her dying had become her singular focus. As we chatted and prayed, it was obvious that, although her gaze was in my direction, I was not the object of her attention. Her interest was beyond me, past me, through me, behind me, beside me. Even though my mother was fully orientated and conscious, she appeared to be intently listening to someone whom I could not see or hear. She would frequently smile and nod as though taking directions, perhaps those that she needed for her immediate future. On one such occasion I dared ask, "Mom, is Daddy here?" She smiled. I asked whether my son Billy was present. She nodded and chided me for my lack of trust in what I already knew to be true. I asked her to give him a message. She told me he had already heard me and that he was right beside me.

As her time on the earth plane drew to a close, the presence of other family members who had already crossed over was unmistakable. The occasional waft of rose fragrance when no fresh roses were present was puzzling. Not until my journey from her bedside to my own home did I recall dreaming that my son would be at my side when I smelled roses. Tears of joy and gratitude flowed with the awareness of his gentle and unassuming presence.

My father was more vociferous in announcing his attendance. The force of a hand on my shoulder and a voice distinctively like that of my father's, commanding me to "wake up," left no doubt of his presence. His four o'clock in the morning shove alerted me that my mother was in a precarious situation. Her head and upper body were tangled between the bedrails, and she had been desperately trying, without avail, to gain my attention.

The assurance that my son and father were present and offering assistance helped me to help my mother to be fully engaged in preparing for her time of transition. They were there to meet her needs, but their presence added another dimension to my own healing. After my son's death I had an intense longing to mend my family circle. For years my life felt broken, and my family seemed incomplete. Someone was always missing; nothing, it seemed, could fill the void. My father's and son's presence at my mother's side and her sharing of dreams of other family members who came to offer support as she crossed over proved to be the glue that my soul needed to weld generational bonds and mend our family circle.

DR. JANE A. SIMINGTON, PH.D

This healing shift helped me to decide to leave my mother's death bed to meet a need of my own. Gratitude swelled as I prepared for the final good-bye. Flashes of memory and insights of all that my mother had given me and of all that she had taught me flooded my consciousness. In those moments I was cognizant that I had picked this particular mother for the particular lessons that my soul could learn from her. From within that depth of awareness I chose to free her of any karmic bonds that we may have developed in this life as well as any karmic bonds that we may still have attached from previous incarnations. Barely had my thoughts been formulated when a meditation for cutting karmic bonds flooded my consciousness. Chanting the phrases I could remember and using my breath to connect to the Universal Light, I made the intention to draw violet rays toward me:

> I Am the Violet Flame in action in me now.
> I Am the Violet Flame to light alone I bow.
> I Am the Violet Flame blazing like a sun.
> I Am the mighty power of God, freeing everyone.[4]

Within seconds a vibrant violet light entered the crown of my head, shot through my body, and made its way out the soles of my feet. In awe and acceptance, I chanted again. This time a vibrant violet light formed and swelled within my heart centre, pulsated there momentarily, then steadily moved from me and toward my mother. This light bathed her body and flooded the entire bed. As a purple smoke, it moved to fill the entire room.

I chanted again. As if in response, the violet light began to retrace its path back toward my mother and then back to me. Settling in my heart, the violet light flickered, and as gently as it had come, it faded.

Bathed in a warm glow and filled to overflowing with a sense of peace, I knew without the slightest doubt that the violet mirage had gently, yet completely severed karmic bonds. My mother was no longer tied to me in any way other than in the way of eternal love. No unfinished business remained. Nothing would need to be mourned. Turning from her and kissing her sleeping form one last time, I whispered words of unconditional love. As I closed the door behind me, I knew that my mother could now journey more lightly. Of this I was sure.

It was two days later, at five in the morning, when my husband received the news. I said little to him; there was little to say. But as I made my way back to my bed, I addressed my mother: "Mom, I would have thought that after all we had been through together, you would have come to tell me yourself. I did not think I would receive this information from Bill."

I was instantly in a dream state, witnessing my mother and father walking side by side. They were dressed for travel. Mother wore a white blouse and blue skirt, an outfit she herself had made. She carried a small cloth satchel. Daddy's grey woven hat was one I remembered well. They entered from the east, coming in to a large, gothic-style building. I immediately thought that this building was like a train station I had seen in Europe.

Aware of being placed by a guiding presence behind a large pillar, I knew, even in the dream state, that this dream was not about me; I was being allowed to witness privileged information.

As my parents moved forward from east to west, they passed a ticket wicket. Mother glanced at my dad. He shook his head, indicating that they did not require tickets. They proceeded to the far end of the building and stopped directly in front of two weigh scales. Again, my mother turned to inquire of my father. This time he shrugged his shoulders, suggesting that it was up to her. Placing her satchel on the floor, she stepped on one of the scales. Glancing at the reading, she turned to again inquire of my father. He shook his head to indicate "No." Mother nodded, seeming to understand. Picking up the satchel, she took my dad's arm, and together they turned to enter a tunnel-like opening in the northwest end of this gigantic room. Although I did not witness a train or any other vehicle of travel, I knew that they were leaving via some mode of transportation that would take them on the next phase of the journey.

The instant that I could no longer see them, the dream ended, and I was fully awake. I knew I had been granted a vision and had been privileged with an incredible gift.

Yet I pondered the scales. What was the symbolism? For days I feverously searched the Internet and dream dictionaries. Finally, the clue I needed: "weight or weightless." My mother had been in and out of her body so many times during her preparation for transition. Getting on the scale and finding herself weightless affirmed that she would not be returning to the physical world. My father's confirming nod indicated that there was no doubt that she was now in spirit form.

As with most dream symbols, the more you work with them, the more you are able to discover deeper layers of meaning, and so it was with the symbol of the scales. A few days following our mother's funeral, my sister reminded me of the story of the scales in Egyptian mythology as described in the Book of the Dead. According to that teaching, at the time of death the soul is weighed against a feather to determine the guilt that is carried. A guiltless soul is ready to move forward into the afterlife.

Some months later I travelled to the British Isles. While in Ambleside, England, I visited the church of St. Mary's at Rydal, a little stone church William Wordsworth had been instrumental in building. Inscribed on one of the stones in a small welcoming circle were the words "What is it to cease breathing, but to free the breath from its restless tides that it may rise and expand and seek God unencumbered?" A tingle raced up my spine as the words entered my consciousness. I knew that my Mother's scales had been balanced against the feather. I knew that she had left behind the restless tides so that she could rise and expand and seek God unencumbered. Of this I was sure.

I offer my mother's dream narratives as well as my own and the spiritual transformation that occurred for both of us as we journeyed side by side during her dying as a gift of hope to those who are preparing to leave this dimension. I also trust that in the relating of the sacred moments that my mother and I shared, others will find the courage to be more fully present to the dream life and other spiritual experiences that are unfolding before them when loved ones are ending their time on this plane.

To find and role-model courage is essential when being present to the soul-concerns that surface during a time of dying, for many fear things of a spiritual nature. A great teacher once told me that to overcome fear, we must embrace it. To embrace fear, we must look it straight in the face and challenge it. The teacher advised that if we want to come to know more intimately the realm of the spiritual worlds and be more open to seeing, sensing, and receiving the guidance that is being offered on a moment-to-moment basis, we must stop responding as though we are only physical beings without a spiritual essence.

Years ago, as a nurse who was beginning to work with palliative patients, I studied ways to assist in the dying process. The resources described the experiences similar to my mother's as hallucinatory and attributed them to drug effects or a lack of brain oxygenation. These teachings stem from a paradigm that views death as the ending of physical life, with no acknowledgement of the incredible spiritual process that is unfolding. Such messages have not only instilled fear of death and dying, but also interfered with the care that a human soul requires as it makes its transition from this reality to the next.

When we disregard the spiritual component of dying and death and view the dreams and visions of those who are dying as hallucinations, there is little reason to acknowledge dreams as messages from the spirit world. Whenever I hear someone trying to explain away the spiritual experiences of dying and grieving people, I recall that ancient people viewed dreams as the vehicle through which the gods spoke to them. Carl Jung's words on dream awareness reiterate these beliefs. Jung noted that a dream that we do not bother to interpret is like a letter from the gods that we have not bothered to read.[5] I sometimes remind people who are having difficulty seeing dreams as spiritual messages that all the major religions share dream narratives. When I teach about death and care of the dying, I ask students to explore various spiritual texts for dream references and often ask such questions as "Why is it that we believe an angel appeared to Joseph, telling him to take the child and his mother and flee to Egypt, yet we are unable to transfer such beliefs to our own lives and therapeutic practices?"[6]

Even though there is considerable evidence in favor of using dream work as a therapeutic tool, many helpers shy away from exploring the dreams of another, stating they lack an ability to accurately interpret dreams.[7,8] James Hillman emphasized that it is not necessary,[9] and often not even therapeutic, to offer an interpretation of another's dream. Rather, it is the very act of describing the dream to a trusted other that is therapeutic. In verbalizing, the dreamer often remembers hidden aspects of the dream and gains added insights and guidance.

Willingness to tiptoe into the spiritual terrain requires a certain level of vulnerability and risk taking. Willingness to risk on our own behalf and on behalf of a soul companion who is making a transition back to the spirit world is an essential part of soulful caring.

I was determined to do all that I could to assist my mother into freedom, even during moments when that required being vulnerable and deeply honest. How will you walk beside your loved ones during those hours when their physical bodies are dying? How will you assist in freeing their spirits?

CHAPTER 13

# LIVING A TRANSFORMED LIFE

*The best way to predict your future is to create it.*
Abraham Lincoln

Poet and philosopher John O' Donahue noted:

> When your soul awakens, you begin to truly inherit your life. You leave
> the kingdom of fake surface, repetitive talk and weary roles and slip deep
> into the true adventure of who you are and who you are called to become.[1]

Once you awaken, you never want to return to your old patterns. You are
no longer willing to squander your essence on undertakings that do not
nourish your true self. You become impatient for growth and change, and
you long to use your gifts and talents.[2] "You want your God to be wild and
to call you to where your destiny awaits."[3] And yet, although we know the
truth of what O'Donahue taught, we fear the changes that we need to make
in ourselves and in our relationships to someday arrive at that place, the
place of divine wildness. Is it perhaps true, as Marion Williamson[4] stated
that our greatest fear is not that we are unworthy, but that we are powerful
beyond measure? What could we be, what could we do if we truly reclaimed
our power, if we really allowed our wings to unfurl, if we really took flight?

In *The Prayer of Jabez*, Bruce Wilkinson[5] wrote of this fear. He explained
for the modern mind the Old Testament prayer of Jabez:

> While Jabez was always more honorable than his brothers, he suffered
> under the burden of his name. His mother had called him Jabez, meaning,
> I bore him in pain. Finally Jabez called out to the God of Israel begging to

be as blessed as his brothers. He petitioned God saying, Oh, that You would bless me indeed, that You would enlarge my territory, that Your hand would be with me, and that You would keep me from evil, that I may not cause pain! So God granted him what he requested.[6]

Wilkinson explained that many of us do not believe we are worthy of all the good things our Creator wants to give us, so we never ask to be blessed indeed! To be blessed indeed is to be greatly and generously blessed. When we ask to be blessed indeed, we recognize the goodness of our Creator and our Divine Birth Right to the fullest of blessings. Wilkinson delineated that, as Jabez, it is not only our right, but also our responsibility to ask to be blessed indeed and to have our territory expanded. We have been given a mandate to expand, here on Earth, the glory of our Maker. We have received incredible talents and abilities to accomplish this goal. We have been told not to hide our talents under a bushel, but to use them for the good and the betterment of *all*.[7]

Acknowledgement of our mandate to "spread the kingdom" comes with an incredible awareness of the largeness of the task we have agreed to undertake. Spreading the kingdom is about spreading goodness and bringing others into awareness of who they really are. When we recognize and willingly claim this responsibility we, as did Jabez, know of our need to call for the hand of our Creator to continually work through us and direct us. We know that this commitment will lead into unfamiliar territory. We know that on our own we will fail, for the task unfolding before us is too momentous for us to succeed unaccompanied and unprotected. Yet we trust that our Creator will work through us and protect us. This then becomes our armor, not the fear of old.

Like Jabez, and also like Job,[8] many of us have been torn apart on the rough seas of life. We not only have numerous fears about moving forward, but also hold considerable doubts about how we are to do so and what first steps we are to take to make our new reality a possibility.

Several centuries ago Dante Alighieri[9] began his magisterial epic on existence, *The Commedia*, with these words:

In the middle of the road of my life
I awoke in a dark wood
Where the true way was wholly lost.

Dante taught that the journey begins in the middle of our life and when we finally awake from our long slumber, we get in touch with a part of ourselves that we barely experienced—our core—our soul. Not recognizing where we are, it feels like we are waking in the dark.

A number of years ago I was at this place in the dark woods, feeling as though I had been taken apart and put together wrong, knowing that I had once been very good at many things. I was now uncertain of my talents and gifts or even whether I had any. My husband, in his solid and logical way, asked me to tell him what success for me would look like. It was a challenging question, one I was unable to answer, yet one I pondered for many, many months.

How could I define success when I had no idea of who I was, who I was becoming, or what I was going to be good at? As Jabez did, I began to beg. I reshaped his prayer to better suit my life and circumstances and then recited it daily: "Oh God, bless me indeed. Expand my territory. Let Your hand be on me always, leading me, guiding me, and protecting me so I may do incredible good by empowering self-love." During my morning wailing-walks I added a plea to be shown my gifts and talents: "I identify and fully use all of my talents and creative abilities in the most successful and abundant ways."

During that intense time of searching I walked my first labyrinth. Years previously, I had viewed the labyrinth in Chartres Cathedral near Paris, France, and at that time it had meant little to me. Now, however, an advertisement that announced an upcoming labyrinth workshop triggered my need to know the teachings surrounding this spiritual tool.

A labyrinth is in the form of a circle with a meandering but purposeful path from the edge to the centre and back out again. Each labyrinth has only one path, and as you enter it, the path becomes a metaphor for your journey through life, sending you first to your "center" and then back out to the edge of your path. Walking the labyrinth is a spiritual process meant to awaken us to the deep rhythm within ourselves and to identify the oneness in ourselves with the path we are taking.

Based upon the circle, the universal symbol of unity and wholeness, the labyrinth sparks the human imagination and introduces us to kaleidoscopic patterning that builds a sense of relationship, one person to another, to many people, to the whole of creation. It enlivens the intuitive parts of our nature and stirs within us the longing for connectedness and the remembrance of our purpose for living.[10]

A labyrinth is a long-hidden mystical means of tapping into sources of inner wisdom. It is a richly inspired instrument, a pilgrimage that focuses our attention in a powerful way and connects our spirit to its creative energies.[11, 12] Many are once again using the ancient wisdom found in the labyrinth as a meaningful spiritual tool, as a way to strengthen the voice within to more clearly identify the path without.

Walking the labyrinth during the course of that weekend resulted in insights of great value at that particular turning point in my life. Although during the initial walk I did not feel anything odd, special, sacred, or spiritual, I was astounded when I later reread my journal. I was also amazed to discover that, following each entry, I had written, "And is that okay?"

In a first notation I commented that, when I entered the labyrinth, numerous others were also walking; yet by the time I finished, I was the lone journeyer. Reflection resulted in the acknowledgement that, indeed, during much of my life, especially the years of healing and growth, I had walked alone. As I pondered the "Is that okay?" question, I felt a surge of gratefulness for all the lessons I had garnered as I travelled, mainly unaccompanied, into unfamiliar soul terrain. Aware that my life's path was leading in a direction of leadership, yet with little idea of what that truly meant, I sensed that the solitary path was somehow preparing me for what lay ahead.

A second entry offered further insight. Although you are not supposed to be able to get lost in a labyrinth because the path leads only one way, about a third of the way through I found myself retracing my steps. My son died during my third decade. The journal entry left little doubt of the metaphorical reminder that retracing those labyrinth steps reflected my soul's journey during those difficult years when I had wandered dispiritedly lost, in the darkest of wildernesses. The constant search for what I had lost and the search for the right path out of that darkness were always overshadowed by my desperate need to retrace every step, to reexamine every aspect of my life in an attempt to discover what I had done that had caused me to be plunged into the unbearable abyss. As I reflected on the "Is that okay?" question, I humbly honored the soul growth that had taken place during those dark nights of intense pain and searching. For, although I wished that there could have been another way for me to learn the soul lessons that my time of sorrow brought, I knew the great value that the lessons had rendered. Even back then, while I was still carrying much grief,

numerous times I would feel an overwhelming and deep sense of gratefulness for the soul gifts I had received as I journeyed through those difficult
days and nights.

I knew that my healing had contributed to my ability and comfort to
walk outside the path; "on the edge," so to speak. Those particular entries
made me smile, but they also brought to conscious awareness how accurately the labyrinth had revealed my life's journey. There was little doubt
that some viewed my personal healing and the work that I was then beginning as "a bit on the edge" and others as "way over the top." As if in answer
to the journal question "And is that okay?" I picked up Martin Wallace's little booklet, *Celtic Reflections*. His words assured me that being on the edge
was okay! I particularly loved and memorized "At the edge we see horizons
denied to those who stay in the middle"[13] and "Walking along a cliff-top,
our bodies and souls face each other and that is how we grow."[14]

I decided the edge was where I needed to be. My prayer, which had
once been to again belong to the mainstream of life, became instead a prayer
to remain on the spiritual edge. I decided to make my life a purposeful pilgrimage, not an aimless trail.[15] I knew that to maintain this spiritual edge I
could not rely on the spiritual experiences of my past.[16] I needed to find
more and more ways to make the pilgrimage into the core of my being in
discovery of my own divinity.

All of my early life I had been a devote Roman Catholic, and I expected
that any experiences that would allow me to taste more completely the spiritual moments in life would be those that would enhance my relationship
with Jesus. Holding those expectations, I perceived a question posed by a
graduate student, "Was Jesus shaman or priest?" as not only meaningless,
but also sacrilegious. How could there possibly be any association between
Jesus and the notions of Shamanism? Yet her pondering sparked a deep,
unexplainable yearning in me to seek the answer—a yearning that rapidly
and unmercifully flung me headfirst into an in-depth study of Shamanism
and Celtic spirituality. The discoveries within these systems brought me face
to face with numerous religious-based fears and propelled me into a major
belief crisis, but the reawakening to this ancient wisdom became a powerful
catalyst for an even more intense exploration of esoteric knowledge buried
deep within other religions and spiritual practices. Although I did not find
the Jesus of my childhood, I discovered the "fruit salad of religions" that
Thich Nhat Hanh described in the opening chapter of his book, *Living Bud-*

*dha, Living Christ*. Like him, I discovered that "fruit salad can be delicious!" Like Thich Nhat Hanh, "I do not see any reason to spend one's whole life tasting just one kind of fruit. We human beings can be nourished by the best values of many traditions."[17]

A decade or so later I was again reminded of the fruit salad concept. A new Buddhist temple had opened in my city, and was invited to give a keynote address at its interfaith conference. The night before the event I had a vivid dream in which I witnessed my mother in a large art museum. With a brochure in hand, she was viewing a long row of goddess-like statues. Recalling her devotion during her lifetime to the Catholic version of the "Mother of God," I motioned for her to observe a most beautiful statue of the Virgin Mary. Seemingly surprised at my invitation, she responded, "Oh, I know all about her; now I need to learn about these." The following morning I related this dream at the interfaith conference. I did so feeling confident that my mother was affirming the theological fruit salad I had been making. I believed that she was encouraging me not only to share with that group, but also to continue blending the various theologies I had studied to bring healing and peace to those with whom I work. I concluded that presentation paraphrasing Thich Nhat Hanh.

People kill and are killed because they hold too tightly to their own ideologies, believing theirs is the only right and true way. Practice nonattachment from views in order to consider other's viewpoints. This is the clearest path to peace.[18]

Throughout *Living Buddha, Living Christ*, Thich Nhat Hanh reminded his readers that the sacred is not static. Positioning ourselves on the edge, means recognizing that the linear, logical, frame-by frame thinking, created by accepting only one way of viewing the sacred, is no longer a roadmap we can trust. There are many paths to the Divine. For most of us, the longest and most difficult one, because it is the one most wrought with deeply engrained fears, is the path that leads to the rediscovery of our own Divinity. Only after we are thus enlightened can we relate to the Divinity within others, and only then can we recognize and respond to the Divine within all of Creation. To come to Know and to be One with the Divine in All, is the object of our spiritual search.

As we each in our own lives come to honor the Divine within ourselves and within all that has been created, we acknowledge the great need to be responsive to the planet and the ecological imbalance that is taking place.

There is a great need for each of us to hear and respond to the Great Cry, the cry to live in oneness, which for the last four or more centuries has been all but obliterated.

As the members of the UN Environmental Sabbath Program have declared:

> We have become estranged from the movements of the Earth.
> We have turned our backs on the cycles of life.
>
> We have forgotten who we are.[19]

We must once again remember. We must once again acknowledge as Chief Seattle did:[20]

> We did not weave the web of life,
> We are merely a strand in it.
>
> Whatever we do to the web,
> We do to ourselves.

There is a great need to restore the ancient teachings and practices that once consecrated the universal marriage of matter and spirit. The call is loud to rethink the dualism that separates the sacred and the secular, the natural and the supernatural, body and soul.

Little by little, more and more of the Earth's people are hearing her cry and responding. More and more of us are remembering, "We are nature. Long have we been absent.... We have circled and circled till we have arrived home again."[21] In coming full circle, more and more of her children are reconnecting to the transformational power of the landscape, the elements, and the directions. As we do so, many of us feel bewildered by the deep and intense need to create sacred ceremony and practice sacred rituals that honor this connection. Many believe that they have no Indigenous roots, and thus ponder the source of such attachments and longings. In truth, however, each of us has tribal roots, pagan roots. The Earth is Mother to each of us. Her Landscape, Her Rocks, Her Water, Her Fire, Her Air are for each of us, belong fully to each of us, are within each of us. It is time to honor again, as our ancestors did, the Earth as our body. Her Water is our blood. Air is our breath, and Fire is our spirit.

Since the dawn of civilization humans have lived in close attunement with the elemental forces in nature. The Chinese honored five primal elements: Fire, Earth, Metal, Wood, and Water. The Greeks identified the

Earth's energies as Earth, Air, Fire, and Water. Some Indigenous tribes included Sound in their elemental diagrams.[22] These were not simply metaphors; they were experienced as real. Individual and communal life was structured around the need to maintain balance between the elements and forces of nature. Personal and collective power was drawn from these sources as well as from the rivers, the mountains, the lightning and thunder, the sun, the moon, and the sky. The need to stay in right relationship with these forces was a common celebration theme, especially in honoring the power-point times of the year, such as during the new and full moons, the summer and winter solstices, and the autumn and spring equinoxes.

Connecting with the elements of the Earth helps us more readily connect with the season and the cycles within our own lives: spring, summer, autumn, winter, birth, growth, decline, and death. As we change and grow, the seasons offer constant reminders of the transformational forces all around us. Meditative visualizations can remind us to pay close attention to this connection.

*Recall a spring morning. Smell the freshness. Ponder the power contained within one breath; remember where your breath comes from. Breathe deeply as you acknowledge that your breath is connecting you to the Great All.*

*Breathe in the purples from the mountains; as you do so, experience the purples of the mountains fill you with strength. Fill every cell with purple. Breathe in the blues from the Oceans. Experience the balancing effect.*

*Feel the waters of the oceans gently rocking your body.*

*Breathe in the greens from the forests. Feel the growth, the newness; feel the freshness.*

*Breathe in the yellows, reds, and oranges from the soil and from the prairies. Experience the yellows, reds, and oranges in every cell of your body. Experience the productivity of summer and autumn as it fills your being.*

*Breathe in the cold air of winter. How many winters have you carried on your back? Breathe in gratefulness for each, for the lessons each hardship taught you.*

*One more time sense the feeling of spring all around you. Breathe in the spring air. Feel the freshness, the newness. Feel the transformation that the movement through each of the seasons has brought to you.*

Becoming more aware of the Earth's processes and seeing ourselves as part of the whole helps us to let go of our need to control life. We are reminded to accept the seasons and changes as a part of the unfolding of the universe within and around us. Just as the fertility and newness of spring have been celebrated for tens of thousands of years, we too can plant the seeds of newness, the ones we sorted during the days and nights of our long and bitter winters. We too can feel our own power as we rise to greet the sun in the summer-solstice mornings. We too can gather the fruits of our harvest as we once again prepare for our quiet times in hibernation.

Being thus connected, we are more able to recognize that there are really no beginnings and no endings. Being thus connected, we recognize that even in death there is no real separation.

> Do not stand at my grave and weep
> I am not there, I do not sleep.
>
> I am a thousand winds that blow.
> I am the diamond glint on snow.[23]

The Navajo remind us that when we transform ourselves, we transform everything around us. To do so, we must celebrate and bring beauty blessings wherever we are. In many traditions water, ashes, salt, rocks, crystals, and other amulets are blessed and used to protect and to remind us of the sacred in all things.

Blessings are also sent in prayer form. This little blessing message from my aging Mother is an example.

A number of years ago, while I was visiting her, a tragic event occurred in the small town where she lived. The event itself and the circumstances surrounding it fueled deep anger within me. Witnessing my emotional turbulence, mother asked me to "simply bless the situation." I inquired how she could say such a thing when innocent people had been harmed. She responded, "You simply never know all the details; only God can know." She went on to explain that we can never fully know or understand why people behave the way they do. Nor can we know why people are affected by the behaviors of others in the ways they are. She emphasized:

> By the time you are my age you will have seen many things, and if you have been paying attention, you will have learned two important lessons. The first is that there is always more than one side to every fight. The second is that difficult life circumstances have a way of eventually producing some good results.

The deep truth within her message could not be denied.

Mother taught me that when she heard sad and hurtful news, she would immediately send a blessing to the one who had been hurt. Next she blessed the one who had done the harm. She then sent a huge blessing to anyone who had witnessed or heard of the tragedy, herself included.

Mother knew that the pain and sorrow and hurt of another affects each of us in various and numerous ways. So, last, she would send a blessing out into the world, knowing that even the "sun and the moon and the stars are affected when human beings suffer."

I received with an open heart the gift my mother gave me, and to this day I try diligently to follow her blessing-practices. When I do, I am immediately released from any need to own or overly invest in the situation. I have found the act of blessing to be a great "shield" that surrounds me during those first moments of hearing tragic news. This does not mean that I am unsympathetic to another's distress; nor does it mean that I do not work diligently to make changes when I can. It does mean that the circumstances of others no longer paralyze or drain me emotionally. It also means that when I need to take action, I have already sent a healing blessing to those I will be working with. When that happens, the blessing has already been working as a beacon of light, helping to clear the path toward healing. Let us each add our voice to the Navajo blessing. "May it be beautiful all around me."[24]

In sending blessings, we become an active participant in transforming the social, cultural, religious, and spiritual practices around us, which opens the gates for wholeness to again be honored. To transform in the direction of wholeness is to acknowledge that healing ourselves and working to resolve the contradictions in the Human-Earth ecology is the same work.[25] It is recognition of the Divine within All. To resolve this contradiction is to stand on the edge and affirm that the "Earth *is* Christos, *is* Buddha, *is* Allah, *is* Gaia."

May the God within and without bless your journey to oneness, your journey of transformation. I send this blessing to guide your way:

May our Creator speak to you through creation.
May you be carried by the tides and the waves.
May you find yourself in the unfolding of the seasons,
Until you rest at last among the clouds.

# CHAPTER REFERENCES

## Chapter 1: Experiencing Parallel Realities (3-15)

1. Burkhardt, M. A., & Nagai- Jacobson, M. G. 2002. *Spirituality: Living our Connectedness*. Albany: Delmar/Thomson Learning.

2. Coyle, J. 2002. Spirituality and health: Toward a framework for exploring the relationship between spirituality and health. *Journal of Advanced Nursing* 37(6), 589-597.

3. Simington, J. 1996. The response of the human spirit to loss. *Living With Our Losses Bereavement Magazine* 1(1), 9-11.

4. The Bible. *Book of Exodus*.

5. Kuhn, T. 1962. *Structure of Scientific Revolution*. Chicago: University of Chicago Press.

6. Jung, C. G. 1959. *Psychology and Religion: West and East*. Translation, R. F. C. Hull. Princeton: Princeton University Press.

7. Jung, C. 1934/1968. *Archetypes and the Collective Unconscious*. Princeton: Princeton University Press.

8. Balinese Guide. 1999. *Personal Communication*. Bali, Indonesia.

9. Ibid. Balinese Guide. 1999.

10. Hope, J. 1997. *Secret Language of the Soul: A Visual Guide to the Spiritual World*. San Francisco: Chronicle Books.

11. Johnson, P. G. 1997. *God and World Religions: Basic Beliefs and Themes*. Shippensburg, PA: Ragged Edge Press.

12. Ibid. Balinese Guide. 1999.

13. Simington, J. 2003. *Journey to the Sacred: Mending a Fractured Soul*. Edmonton, AB: Taking Flight Books.

14. Kelsey, M. 1992. *Dreamquest: Native American Myth and the Recovery of Soul.* Rockport, MA: Element.

15. O'Hara, M. 1943. *My Friend Flicka.* New York: Perennial Library: Harper Row.

16. Simington, J. and Victorian Order of Nurses. 1999. *Listening to Soul Pain* (Audiovisual). Edmonton, AB: Taking Flight Books.

17. Rugh, M. 2001. Art, nature, and aging: A Shamanic perspective. In M. Farrelly-Hansen (Ed.). *Spirituality and Art Therapy: Living the Connection.* New York: Jessica Kingsley Publishers.

18. Boehm, R., Golec, J., Krahn, R., & Smyth, D. 1999. *Life Lines: Culture, Spirituality and Family Violence.* Edmonton, AB: University of Alberta Press.

## Chapter 2: Moving Beyond Fear (16-31)

1. Williamson, M. 1992. *A Return to Love.* New York: Harper Perennial.

2. Simington, J. 2003. *Journey to the Sacred: Mending a Fractured Soul.* Edmonton, AB: Taking Flight Books.

3. Freke, T., & Gandy, P. 2001. *The Jesus Mysteries.* London: Thorsons.

4. Freke, T., & Gandy, P. 2001. *Jesus and the Lost Goddess: Secret Teachings of the Original Christians.* New York: Three Rivers Press.

5. Picknett, L., & Prince, C. 1997. *The Templar Revelation: Secret Guardians of the True Identity of Christ.* Corgi Books. London.

6. Baigent, M., Leigh, R., & Lincoln, H. 1982. *The Holy Blood and the Holy Grail.* London: Jonathan Cape.

7. Begg, E. 1985. *The Cult of the Black Virgin.* London: Arkana.

8. deRose, P. 1988. *Vicars of Christ: The Dark Side of the Papacy.* London: Bantam Press.

9. Ibid. Simington, J. 2003.

10. Andrews, T. 1998. *Animal Speak.* St. Paul, MN: Llewellyn.

11. Ibid. Simington, J. 2003.

12. Ball, P. 1997. *10,000 Dreams Interpreted.* London: Prospero Books.

13. Whitton, J., & Fisher, J. 1986. *Life Between Lives.* New York: Warner Books.

14. Cranston, S. 1998. *Reincarnation: The Phoenix Fire Mystery.* Pasadena: Theosophical University Press.

15. Freke, T., & Gandy, P. 2001. *The Jesus Mysteries.* London: Thorsons.

16. Freke, T., & Gandy, P. 2001. *Jesus and the Lost Goddess: Secret Teachings of the Original Christians.* New York: Three Rivers Press.

17. Harper, T. 2004. *The Pagan Christ*. Toronto: Thomas Allen.

18. Shakespeare, W. *Hamlet*, II, ii, 253.

19. The Bible: *Matthew* 13: 9-17.

## Chapter 3: Exploring Alternate Views of Life and Living (32-43)

1. Author and date unknown. What do you see nurse? In J. L. Christiansen, & J.M. Grybowski. 1993. *Biology of Aging*. St. Louis: Mosby.

2. Simington, J. 2004. Ethics for an evolving spirituality. In J. L. Storch, P. Rodney, & R. Starzomski (Eds.). *Toward a Moral Horizon*, pp. 465-484. Toronto: Pearson Canada.

3. Ibid. Simington, J. Ibid 2004, p. 465.

4. Simington, J. 2000. *Stitched together by memories: Legacy and life review.* www.humanehealthcare.com /voll2e/Stitched.html

5. Ibid. Simington, J. 2004.

6. Ibid. Simington, J. 2004, p. 466.

7. Stoll, R. 1989. The essence of spirituality. In V. Carson (Ed.). *Spiritual Dimensions of Nursing Practice*, pp. 4-23. Philadelphia: W. B. Saunders.

8. Simington, J. 1996. Responses of the human spirit to loss. *Living Our Losses Bereavement Magazine*, 1(1)-11.

9. Olson, J. K., Paul, P., Douglass, L., Clark, B. M., Simington, J., & Goddard, N. 2003. *Canadian Journal of Nursing Research*, 35(3), 94-107.

10. Hood-Morris, L. E. 1995. The concept of spirituality in the context of the discipline of nursing. *Unpublished Master's Thesis*, University of BC, Vancouver, BC.

11. Hubert, M. 1969. Spiritual care for every patient. *Journal of Nursing Education* 2, 9-11 and 29-31.

12. Hungelmann, J., Kenkel-Rossi, E., Klassen, L., & Stollenwerk, R. (1985). Spiritual well-being in older adults: Harmonious interconnectedness. *Journal of Religion and Health*, 24 (2), 147-153.

13. Simington, J. 1996. Attitudes toward the old and death, and spiritual well-being. *Journal of Religion and Health* 35(1), 21-32.

14. Ibid. Olson, et al., 2003.

15. Greasley, P., Chiu, L. F., & Gartland, M. 2001. The concept of spiritual care in mental health nursing. *Journal of Advanced Nursing* 33(5), 629-637.

16. Gustafson, D. L. 2003. Embodies knowledge or disembodied knowing. *Canadian Nurse* 99(2), 8-9.

17. Burkhardt, M. A., & Nagai-Jacobson, M. G. 2002. *Spirituality: Living Our Connectedness.* Albany: Delmar/Thomson Learning.

18. Kharitidi, O. 1996. *Entering the Circle: Ancient Secrets of Siberian Wisdom Discovered by a Russian Psychiatrist.* San Francisco: Harper Collins.

19. Rogers, M. 1986. Science of unitary human beings. In V. Malinski (ed.), *Explorations on Martha Roger's Science of Unitary Human Beings.* Norwalk, Conn: Appleton-Century Croft.

20. Malinski, V. 1986. Nursing practice within the science of unitary human beings. In V. Malinski (ed.), *Explorations on Martha Roger's Science of Unitary Human Beings.* Norwalk, Conn: Appleton-Century Croft.

21. Rogers, M. 1970. *An Introduction to the Theoretical Basis of Nursing.* Philadelphia: F. A. Davis.

22. Malinski, V. 1986. The relationship between hyperactivity in children and perception of short wavelength light. In V. Malinski (ed.), *Explorations on Martha Roger's Science of Unitary Human Beings.* Norwalk, Conn: Appleton-Century Croft.

23. Carroll, L. & Tober, J. 1999. *Indigo Children.* Carlsbad, CA: Hay House.

24. Virtue, D. 1999. Gifted or troubled. In L. Carroll, & J. Tober (Eds.). *Indigo Children.* Carlsbad, CA: Hay House Carr, (p. 23).

25. Tappe, N. A. 1982. *Understanding Your Life Through Color.* Carlsbad, CA: Starling Publishers.

26. Ibid Rogers, M. 1970.

27. Kuhn, T. 1962. *Structure of Scientific Revolution.* Chicago, Ill: University of Chicago Press.

28. Service, R. (1953). *My Madonna.* In Public Domain.

## Chapter 4: Expanding Definitions of the Spiritual (44-58)

1. Baumann, S. L., & Englert, R. 2003. A comparison of three views of spirituality in oncology nursing. *Nursing Science Quarterly* 16(1), 52-59.

2. Fryback, P. B., & Reinsert, B. R. 1999. Spirituality and people with potentially fatal diagnoses. *Nursing Forum* 34(1), 13-22.

3. Olson, J. K., Paul, P., Douglass, L., Clark, B. M., Simington, J., & Goddard, N. 2003. Addressing the spiritual dimension in Canadian undergraduate nursing education. *Canadian Journal of Nursing Research,* 35(3), 94-107.

4. Hope, J. 1997 *The Secret Language of the Soul: A Visual Guide to the Spiritual World.* San Francisco: Chronicle Books.

5. Hague, W. J. 1995. *Evolving Spirituality.* Edmonton, AB: Department of Educational Psychology, University of Alberta.

6.  Simington, J. 2004. Ethics for an evolving spirituality. In, J. L. Storch, P. Rodney, & R. Starzomski (Eds.). *Toward a Moral Horizon*, pp. 465-484. Toronto: Pearson Canada.

7.  Emblem, J. 1992. Religion and spirituality defined according to current use in nursing literature. *Journal of Professional Nursing 8*(1), 41-47.

8.  Bowker, J. (Ed.).1997. *The Oxford Dictionary of World Religions*. New York: Oxford University Press.

9)  Koenig, H.B., McCullough, E.M., & Larson, D.B. 2001. *Handbook of Religion and Health*. New York: Oxford University Press.

10. Coyle, J. 2002. Spirituality and health: Toward a framework for exploring the relationship between spirituality and health. *Journal of Advanced Nursing 37*(6), 589-597.

11. Dossey, L. 1993. *The Healing Power of Prayer*. San Francisco: Harper.

12. Burkhardt, M. A. and Nagai- Jacobson, M. G. 2002. *Spirituality: Living Our Connectedness*. Albany: Delmar/Thomson Learning.

13. Osterman Fieser, K., & Rogers-Seidl, F. F. 1991. Spiritual distress. In F. F. Rogers-Seidl, (ed.) *Geriatric Nursing Care Plans* pp. 83-87. St. Louis: Mosby Year Book.

14. Ibid. Simington, J. 2004.

15. Frankl, V. E. 1979. *The Unheard Cry for Meaning: Psychotherapy and Humanism*. New York: Touchstone.

16. Simington, J. 2003. *Journey to the Sacred: Mending a Fractured Soul*. Edmonton, AB: Taking Flight Books.

17. Moyers, B. 1993. "Wounded healers." *Bill Moyers: Healing and the Mind*. Prod. David Grubin. PBS Series. New York: Ambrose.

18. Boryshenko, J. 1993. *Fire in the Soul: A New Psychology of Spiritual Optimism*. New York: Warner.

19. Floriani, C. M. 1999. The spiritual side of pain. *American Journal of Nursing 9*(5), 24-25.

20. Gustafson, D. L. 2003. Embodies knowledge or disembodied knowing. *Canadian Nurse 99*(2), 8-9.

21. Simington, J. 1996. The response of the human spirit to loss. *Living With Our Losses Bereavement Magazine 1*(1), 9-11.

22. Campbell, C. 1989. *Meditation with John of the Cross*. Santa Fe: Bear & Co.

23. Simington, J. and Victorian Order of Nurses 1999. *Listening to Soul Pain*. Audiovisual. Edmonton, AB: Taking Flight Books.

24. Boehm, R., Golec, J., Krahn, R., & Smyth, D. 1999. *Life Lines: Culture, Spirituality and Family Violence*. Edmonton, AB: University of Alberta Press.

25. Simington, E. 2003. *Art as Voice for Inner City Adolescents.* Unpublished Master's Thesis. St. Francis Xavier University: Antigonish, NS.

26. Simington, J. 1999-2003. *Journey to Hope and Healing: Beyond Trauma and Abuse.* Simington Consulting: Edmonton, AB.

27. Simington, J. 2012. Multiple losses and the circle of significance. In R. Neimeyer (Ed.). *Techniques of Grief Therapy,* pp. 42-44. New York and London: Routledge Taylor and Francis Group.

28. Ibid. Simington, J., & VON. 1999.

29. Ibid. Simington, J. 2003.

## Chapter 5: Challenge Existing Models of Helping (59-72)

1. Substance Abuse and Mental Health Services Administration. 2007. *Results from the 2006 National Survey on Drug Use and Health: National Findings* (Office of Applied Studies, NSDUH Series H-32, DHHS Publication No. SMA 07-4293). Rockville, MD.

2. McClellan, S. 2001. *Maclean's Magazine,* June 25, 44-45.

3. Maslow, A. H. 1954. *Motivation and Personality.* New York: Harper.

4. Simington, J. 1994. *A Wellness Approach to Life.* Edmonton, AB: Simington Consulting, p. 12.

5. Stoll, R. I. 1989. The essence of spirituality. In V. B. Carson. *Spiritual Dimensions of Nursing Practice.* Philadelphia: W. B. Saunders, pp. 4-23.

6. Simington, J. 1996. The response of the human spirit to loss. *Living With Our Losses Bereavement Magazine* 1(1), 9-11.

7. Hungelmann, J., Kenkel-Rossi, E., Klassen, L. & Stollenwerk, R. (1985). Spiritual well-being in older adults: Harmonious interconnectedness. *Journal of Religion and Health,* 24(2), 147-153.

8. The Bible, *Book of Exodus.*

## Chapter 6: Visioning New Possibilities (73-83)

1. Bentov, I. Stalking the Wild Pendulum. Cited in Ibid Talbot 1991. p.163.

2. Yesh, P. 2000. Personal workshop experience. *Art, Heart and Soul.* Edmonton, AB. www.artheartandsoul.com

3. Einstein, A. & Infeld, L. 1938. *The Evolution of Physics.* New York: Simon & Schuster.

4. McTaggart, L. 2002. *The Field: The Quest for the Secret Force of the Universe.* New York: Harper Collins, p. xiii.

5. Mitchell, E. 1996. *The Way of the Explorer: An Apollo Astronauts Journey through the Material and Mystical Worlds.* London: G. P. Putman, p. 6.

6. Talbot, M. 1991. *The Holographic Universe.* New York: Harper.

7. Ibid. Talbot 1991, pp. 46-47.

8. Ibid. Talbot 1991, pp. 46-47.

## Chapter 7: Achieving Wholeness (84-100)

1. Origen of Alexandria (185-254). *De Principiis* (Early Christian theologian).

2. Andrews, T. 1998. *Animal Speak.* St. Paul, MN: Llewellyn.

3. Emoto, M. 2004. *The Hidden Messages in Water.* Hillsboro, OR: Beyond Words Publishing.

4. Pack, L. & Smith, R. 2009. www.healingrhtyhms.ca

5. De Sousa, A. 2005. The role of music therapy in psychiatry. *Alternative Therapies in Health and Medicine, 11* (6), 52-56.

6. Murrant, G. M., Rykov, M., Amonite, D., & Loynd, M. 2000. Creativity and self care for caregivers. s44-49.

7. Young-Mason, J. 2002.The role of beauty, color, light and nature in the healing process. *Clinical Nurse Specialist, 16*(4), 221-222.

8. Salmon, D. 2001. Music therapy as psycho-spiritual process in palliative care. *Journal of Palliative Care, 17*(3), 142-146.

9. Marr, J. 1998/1999. Guided imagery and music at the end of life: case studies in palliative care. *Journal for the Association of Music and Imagery, 6,* 37-55.

10. LeNevanec, C., & Bridges, L. (Eds.). 2005. *Creating Connections between Nursing Care and the Creative Art Therapies.* Springfield, IL: Charles C. Thomas.

11. Tate, F. B., & Longo, D. A. 2002. Art therapy: Enhancing psychosocial nursing. *Journal of Psychosocial Nursing, 40*(3), 40-47.

12. Williams, Y. 2002. *The Art of Dying: A Jungian View of Patient's Drawings.* Springfield, IL: Charles C. Thomas.

13. Simington, J. 2005. The heart and science of palliative care. *Living Our Losses Bereavement Magazine.* Fall/Winter, pp. 5-9.

## Chapter 8: Being Deeply Rooted in the Sacred (101-113)

1. Cohen, M. J. 1991. *Connecting With Nature.* World Peace University Field Guide. www.mindspring.com

2. Einstein, A. 1931. *Living Philosophies.* New York: Simon & Schuster (pp. 4-5).

3. Adapted from class activity taught by Rugh, M. 2004. *Restoration of the Soul.* Art Therapy Graduate Course. Edmonton, AB: St. Stephen's College. University of Alberta.

4. Ball, P. 1997. *10,000 Dreams Interpreted.* London: Prospero Books.

5. Dickerman, A. C. 1992. *Following Your Path: Using Myths, Symbols, and Images to Explore Your Inner Life.* New York: Putnam.

6. Chetwynd, T. 1982. *Dictionary of Symbols.* Hammersmith, London: Aquarian Press.

7. Simington, J. 1996. *Journey to Healing. Guided Imagery* (audiotape). Edmonton, AB: Taking Flight Books.

8. Freke, T., & Gandy, P. 1999. *The Jesus Mysteries: Was the Original Jesus a Pagan God?* London: Thorsons.

9. Freke, T., & Gandy, P. 2001. *Jesus and the Lost Goddess.* New York: Three Rivers Press.

10. Angus, S. 1925. *Mystery Religions.* London: Dover.

11. Burkert, W. 1987. *Ancient Mystery Cults.* Harvard University Press.

12. Godwin, J. 1981. *Mystery Religions in the Ancient World.* London: Thames & Hudson.

13. Harper, T. 2004. *The Pagan Christ.* Toronto: Thomas Allen.

14. Picknett, L., & Prince, C. 1998. *The Templar Revelation: Secret Guardians of the True Identity of Christ.* London: Corgi Books.

15. Ibid. Freke & Gandy. 1999.

16. Ibid. Harper. 2004

17. Frost, R. 1920. *The Road Not Taken.* Poems by Robert Frost. www.internal.org

## Chapter 9: Re-establishing Sacred Connections (114-130)

1. Roberts, E., & Amidon, E. 1991. *Earth Prayers: From Around the World.* San Francisco: Harper San Francisco.

2. Henderson, S. 1995. *Outback Wisdom.* Sydney: Pan Macmillan Australia Pty.

3. O'Donohue, J. 2008. *To Bless the Space Between Us.* New York: Random House.

4. Rothschild, B. 2000. *The Body Remembers: The Physiology of Trauma and Trauma Treatment.* New York: Norton.

5. Allen, J. G. 1995. *Coping with Trauma.* Washington, DC: American Psychiatric Press.

6. Herman, J. 1997. *Trauma and Recovery.* New York: Basic Books.

7.  Simington, J. 2004. In J. L. Storch, P. Rodney, & R. Starzomski. Ethics for an evolving spirituality. *Toward a Moral Horizon: Nursing Ethics for Leadership and Practice.* Toronto: Person Education Canada. Ch. 23, pp. 465-484.

8.  Boryshenko, J. 1993. *Fire in the Soul: A New Psychology of Spiritual Optimism.* New York: Warner.

9.  Simington, J., & Victorian Order of Nurses. 1999. *Listening to Soul Pain.* Audiovisual. Edmonton, AB: Taking Flight Books.

10. Simington, J. 2005. *Responding Soul to Soul during Times of Spiritual Uprooting.* Edmonton, AB: Taking Flight Books.

11. Boehm, R., Golec, J., Krahn, R., & Smyth, D. 1999. *Life Lines: Culture, Spirituality and Family Violence.* Edmonton, AB: University of Alberta Press.

12. Floriani, C. M. 1999. The spiritual side of pain. *American Journal of Nursing,* 9(5), 24-25.

13. Gustafson, D. L. 2003. Embodied knowledge or disembodied knowing. *Canadian Nurse, 99*(2), 8-9.

14. Lanius, R. A., Williamson, P.C., Densmore, M., Boksman, K., Neufeld, R. W., Gati, J.S., & Menon, R.S. 2004. The nature of traumatic memories: A 4-T fmri functional connectivity analysis. *American Journal of Psychiatry, 161*:36-44.

15. Ibid. Rothschild, B. 2000.

16. van der Kolk, B. A., McFarlane, A. C., & Weisaeth, L. (Eds.). 1996. *Traumatic Stress.* New York: Guilford.

17. Ibid. Rothschild, B. 2000, p. 161.

18. Simington, J. 2007. Four-part process for healing trauma. *Trauma Recovery Certification Program.* Edmonton, AB: Taking Flight International Corporation.

## Chapter 10: Creating Sacred Space (131-140)

1.  Fiore, E. 1995. *The Unquiet Dead.* New York: Ballantine Books.

2.  Ibid. Fiore, 1995.

3.  Simington, J. (2011). *Shielded With Light: A Guide for Cleansing and Sealing Your Aura.* Edmonton, Alberta: Taking Flight Books.

## Chapter 11: Reclaiming Lost Wholeness (141-152)

1.  Simington, J. 2000. *Journey to Hope and Healing: Beyond Trauma and Abuse.* Psycho-educational Program. Edmonton, AB: Simington Consulting.

2.  Herman, J. 1997. *Trauma and Recovery: The Aftermath of Violence from Domestic Violence and Political Terror.* New York, NY: Basic Books.

3. Simington, J. 2003. *Journey to the Sacred: Mending a Fractured Soul*. Edmonton, AB: Taking Flight Books.

4. Wilkinson, T. 1996. *Persephone Returns: Victims, Heroes and the Journey from the Underworld*. Berkley, CA: Pagemill Press.

5. Ibid. Simington, 2003.

6. Simington, J. 2008. *Trauma Recovery Certification Handbook* (4th edition.). Edmonton, AB: Taking Flight International Corporation.

7. Plato, *The Symposium*. Cited in O'Donahue, J. *Reflections from Conamara*. www.johnodonahue.com/reflections. Retrieved March 31, 2009.

8. Simington, J. 2012. *Reintegrating Parts of the Self* (Audiotape). Edmonton, AB: Taking Flight Books.

## Chapter 12: Bringing Peaceful Closure (153-164)

1. Simington, J. 2001. *Stitched Together by Memories: Legacy and Life Review*. www.humanehealthcare.com 1(2).

2. Erickson, E. H. 1963. *Childhood and Society,* 2nd edition. New York: WW Norton & Co.

3. Butler, RN (1982). *Aging and Mental Health: Positive Psychosocial and Biomedical Approaches,* 3rd edition. St. Louis: Mosby.

4. Prophet, E.C. 1991. *Violet Flame, To Heal Body, Mind & Soul*. Corwin Springs MT: Summit University Press.

5. Jung, C G. Seminar on Dream Analysis given 1928-1930. W. McGuire (ed.), *Bollingen Series XCIV*. Princeton: Princeton University Press.

6. The Bible. *Matthew* II (13-15).

7. Bulkeley, K. & Bulkeley, P. 2005. *Dreaming Beyond Death: A Guide to Pre-death Dreams and Visions*. Boston, MA: Beacon Press.

8. Bulkeley, K (Ed.). 2005. *Soul, Psyche, Brain: New Directions in the Study of Religion and Brain-Mind Science*. New York: Palgrave Macmillan.

9. Hillman, J. 1996. *The Soul's Code: In Search of Character and Calling*. New York: Time Warner.

## Chapter 13: Living a Transformed Life (165-174)

1. O'Donahue, J. Retrieved March, 2009. *Reflections for Conamara: The Question Holds the Lantern*. www.jodonahue.com.

2. Ibid. O'Donahue. 2009.

3. Ibid. O'Donahue 2009.

4. Williamson, M. 1992. *A Return to Love: Reflections on the Principals of a Course in Miracles*. New York: Harper Collins, pp.190-191.

5. Wilkinson, B. 2000. *The Prayer of Jabez*. Sisters, Oregon: Multnomah Publishers.

6. The Bible. *Prayer of Jabez:* 1 Chronicles 4:10.

7. The Bible. *Matthew* 5.

8. The Bible. *Chronicles* 1 (4-10).

9. Dante Alighieri, *The Commedia*, cited in Whyte, D. 1994. *The Heart Aroused: Poetry and the Preservation of the Soul in Corporate America*. New York, NY: Currency Doubleday.

10. Artress, L. 1995. *Walking a Sacred Path: Rediscovering the Labyrinth*. New York, NY: Riverhead Books.

11. Ibid. Artress, 1995.

12. Fincher, S. 1991. *Creating Mandalas: For Insight, Healing and Self-Expression*. Boston: Shambhala.

13. Wallace, M. 1970. *Celtic Reflections*. Christchurch, NZ: Tim Tiley Ltd. Ecclesia Books, 18.

14. Ibid. Wallace, 1970, 18.

15. Ibid. Wallace, 1970, 6.

16. Ibid. Wallace 1970, 7.

17. Thich Nhat Hanh, 1995. *Living Buddha Living Christ*. New York, NY: Riverhead Books, 12.

18. Ibid. Thich Nhat Hanh, 1995.

19. UN Environmental Sabbath Program. 1990. *Only One Earth*. Environmental Sabbath Earth Rest Day, June. New York: UN Publication.

20. Chief Seattle, 1890. *Letter to the American Government*. Squamish, BC: Squamish First Nations.

21. Whitman, W. 1819-1892. *We Too, How Long We Were Fooled* (Poem). In Public Domain.

22. Roberts, E. & Amidon, E. 1991. *Earth Prayers*. San Francisco: Harper Collins.

23. Frye, M. E. 1943. *Do Not Stand at My Grave and Weep* (Poem).

24. Navajo chant.

25. Ibid. Roberts & Amidon, 1991, xx1.

35223160R00112

Made in the USA
Charleston, SC
31 October 2014